FROM CHRI
TO CH

CW00500647

*Christianity as the Essence of Humanity in
Rudolf Steiner's Science of the Spirit*

Pietro Archiati

TEMPLE LODGE
London

Translated by Matthew Barton

Temple Lodge Publishing
51 Queen Caroline Street
London W6 9QL

Published by Temple Lodge 1996

Originally published in German under the title *Christentum oder Christus?*
Das Christentum als reines Menschentum in der Geisteswissenschaft Rudolf
Steiners by Verlag am Goetheanum, Dornach, Switzerland, 1995

A catalogue record for this book is available from the British Library

ISBN 0 904693 83 X

Cover by S. Gulbekian. Art: *The Transfiguration* by Raphael
Typeset by DP Photosetting, Aylesbury, Bucks
Printed and bound in Great Britain by Cromwell Press Limited,
Broughton Gifford, Wiltshire

CONTENTS

FORWORD

Many people have asked me, through the years, to make some of my ideas and thoughts available to a wider audience by writing them down. I have always had an inner resistance to doing this, for a simple reason: once things are printed in black and white, the reader has an expectation that they represent the 'whole' truth. At the same time, the author is no longer in a position to alter things—to illuminate and characterize them from a different angle by expanding or adding. Truth is, after all, inexhaustible. Things can always be viewed from new angles. Or the same thought can be expressed in quite different ways...

If I now undertake to set down some of my thoughts on paper—on a theme which is of enormous importance, and in a form which aims to be accessible to all—it is in the hope that the reader and I can strike the following bargain: I, for my part, have tried to express my ideas and thought-processes without any recourse to absolute and dogmatic formulations. (It goes without saying, though, since reality is always objective as well as inexhaustible, that I have tried to give voice only to what is objective and true.) The reader, for his part, should not forget that there are aspects which this book does *not* express. The thoughts I have written down are intended to help the reader himself draw out those I have not. If I could *converse* with my reader, his own thoughts would allow me to expand my theme with ever new aspects. After all, it was through conversation—the Platonic Dialogues—that western thinking was born.

This book developed out of two lectures about world religions which I gave at the Summer Conferences at the Goetheanum in Switzerland in 1995. After the publisher asked me to make my thoughts available to a wider audience, I expanded the material and considerably broadened its scope. The form and content, though, retain something of the atmosphere of an open lecture; this is actually my intention. I do not consider it a disadvantage if formal perfection is sacrificed to greater immediacy.

I hope that those who have little or no familiarity with Rudolf Steiner's science of the spirit—and this book is also written with such readers in mind—will forgive me one thing: it was beyond the scope of this volume to explain and elaborate on much that underlies it; particularly, for example, in the chapter on Jesus of Nazareth. I must ask such readers to refrain from hasty judgement, and to simply take my thoughts in good faith as information about this spiritual science—and above all as testimony to the central position which the Being of Christ occupies within it.

I feel I owe the reader a further word about my own relationship to the work of Rudolf Steiner. Anyone not familiar with his science of the spirit must inevitably wonder why such unique significance is attributed to this one person. It smacks, surely, of dogmatism or fanaticism. I can only counter this by asking the reader himself to judge whether, in unfolding my own ideas and thoughts, I seem to him to be dogmatic. Neither he nor I can call upon a higher authority than our own power of judgement.

I would like to thank two people in particular for helping to make this book possible: Vreni Läng and Joseph Morel. They overcame my disinclination towards writing and, for the reader's sake, took down the words I dictated to them.

Pietro Archiati

1
WHAT IS 'CHRISTIANITY'?

Christianity occupies a very special place within Rudolf Steiner's science of the spirit. He views it, on the one hand, as a synthesis of all religions; but it is also, on the other hand, just one historical phenomenon alongside other religions. To differentiate between these two aspects is of paramount importance.

What we commonly think of as Christianity is the cultural form it has adopted in the last two thousand years. This is composed chiefly of *human* thoughts and dogmas, *human* institutions, churches and denominations; in other words everything which *human beings* have developed in relation to the Christ Event.

The Christian 'religion' has always sought to take the Being of Christ as its starting point. But it is a fundamental tenet of spiritual science that direct communication between human beings and a real, living world of spirit, increasingly faded; and that, instead, the human 'practice' of religion became more and more prominent. There was less and less real experience and awareness of Christ's own Being and Deeds, while the actions of people and of the Church gained ever greater significance. That is why we must differentiate between the Christianity which arises from Christ's Deeds and the one which derives from the actions of human beings.

Only a new science *of the spirit* appropriate to our times can help us to focus again upon a real and living experience of the supersensible Being of Christ, and upon His workings within humanity, as the essence of Christianity. Then we can become aware of aspects of His influence in the last two thousand years and in our own time, which we cannot know without spiritual science. Rudolf Steiner has the following to say in this connection:

> There are many ways in which anthroposophy must nowadays serve humanity. One important service is in the realm of religion. There is no need for a new religion to be founded. The impulse and purpose which the earth received when a God passed through the human destiny of birth and death, is an Event which can never be surpassed. It is clear to anyone who understands its origin that no new religion can supersede Christianity. We would have a wrong conception of Christianity if we thought it was possible to found a new religion. But as humanity itself continues to develop and advance in supersensible knowledge, its understanding of the Mystery of Golgotha—and therefore also of the Christ Being—will continually deepen. It is the aim of anthroposophy to contribute to this understanding in ways that, at the present time, it is perhaps alone in being able to. (Lecture of 13 April 1922, GA 211.)*

Inasmuch as Christianity was thought of as one religion among others, it could not yet assume its true form. Christianity is, when rightly understood, nothing less than the religion of humanity itself. The Christ Being is an embodiment of the ideal of all human beings. His influence and working arise out of His very Being, which therefore contains the potential to which all human beings, in all future stages of evolution of man and the earth, can aspire. As such, the essence of Christianity is *Christ Himself.*

According to Rudolf Steiner, this cosmic, divine Being of love—the cardinal Being of the solar system—entered and permeated the earth in order to transform it from a cosmos of wisdom to one of love. The essence of Christianity is what Christ Himself is, and what He made possible for

---

*For references to English publications see p. 127.

every human being through His influence and deeds. As such, it is also the essence of humanity itself.

Why do we speak of a Christ Impulse?

When we turn our attention to the Christ Being, we may ask: Who is Christ? Rudolf Steiner speaks often of His deeds and influence as the Christ *Impulse*. Many people find this disconcerting because it seems impersonal. But Rudolf Steiner considered this of great importance; for him, the word 'impulse' expresses the impossibility of grasping the Christ Event by imagining that Christ works merely in a human, personal way. He says the following about this in his lecture of 17 April 1912 (GA 143):

> But Christianity does not regard Christ as a personality, as some founder of an abstract religious system. Anyone who tries to found a new religion in our day and age, sows only discord. Christian initiation is not based upon personality but upon a fact, an impersonal divine deed, which took place before the eyes of human beings.

Similarly, Rudolf Steiner often speaks of the Mystery of Golgotha as an 'affair of the gods', a cosmic Event in the world of the hierarchies, which human beings could witness because it also had a human, historical aspect.

It is an *impulse*, therefore, that we are concerned with, an all-encompassing Event within nature and humanity, in which cosmic forces entered into full earthly reality. The Mystery of Golgotha is a mystic fact pervading the whole natural, physical world. The scope and nature of the influence of a human being at the present stage of evolution is infinitely more limited than the cosmic and earthly working of the Christ Event.

If we really grasp what is meant by 'impulse', we can also better understand the principal difference between Christianity in this sense and all pre-Christian religions. These were *Father*-God religions and their founders were, albeit very highly evolved, human personalities. Every religion represents one particular form and expression of human beings' striving to be 're-united' (from the Latin *religare*, meaning 're-connect') with the world of spirit. In the same lecture, Rudolf Steiner says:

> The fundamental difference between Christianity and other religions lies in the different nature of its task within the world; its initiation principle, which leads to Christ, is different from that at work in cultures based upon other religious principles. The source of the Christian principle of initiation and its task within cosmic evolution is an event, a fact, not a personality ... a single phrase suffices to characterize—although only outwardly—the source of esoteric Christianity and Christian initiation: the death which was experienced through the uniting of Christ with Jesus of Nazareth. The principle of Christian initiation aims to lead us towards an understanding of that fact, which we call the Mystery of Golgotha.

The pre-Christian religions—*religions* in the true sense of the word—were not the unaided work of human beings. Divine powers guided mankind through the human founders of these religions. Divine impulses were given, which were different for different peoples or cultural epochs. In every case, though, the divine influence worked in a *Father*-God way. Such influence arises from the fact that natural necessity—as expression of the divine Father—is also, initially, all that is at work in the human being; individual freedom only develops later. Even when mention is made of a Trinity, it is understood and experienced as a threefold quality of the *Father*-God. In Hinduism, for example, the divine Trinity of Brahma (the Creator), Vishnu (the Upholder) and Shiva (the Destroyer) is, from a Christian point of view, a trinity within the Father realm. The divine power—in which the human being is embedded—creates, upholds and destroys all things.

The *Son* of God was spoken of in the Mysteries only as One who would come in the future to 'redeem' mankind. In other words, the work of redemption was not ascribed to the Father God. The power of the Father was thought of, ultimately, as grace, as guidance from without; as guidance which works as a natural necessity in which the human being is embedded, with which he conforms. The human being put everything into the hands of divine grace and expected it to fulfill all his needs. Everything of an individual or independent nature was actually considered sinful. Divine influence was seen wholly in terms of the workings of the natural world.

The radically new impulse which entered earth's evolution through the divine *Son*—the 'Evangelium' or 'good news from the world of the hierarchies'—allows the influence of the Father to be fulfilled through human freedom. This is something quite new in evolution. Before Christ, religion was thought of as a return to the divine source, to the lap of God the Father, to the original state of paradise. The Christ Being seeks and offers the opposite; looking forward to the future, He asks us to transform the world of the Father by exercising freedom. Pre-Christian religions did not contain this complete reversal of the Father-principle's natural necessity through the Son's impulse towards freedom. They could not have done, for the Christ Being had not yet united Himself wholly with the earth. In his lecture of 11 September 1924 (GA 346), Rudolf Steiner says:

> If we were to speak only* of God the Father, we would be justified in ... speaking of natural phenomena which are also simultaneously spiritual; for natural phenomena do indeed embody spiritual effects and influences. Our

---

* not 'now' ('nun') as was wrongly transcribed instead of 'only' ('nur')— P.A.

contemporary science originated in—and is still—a one-sided knowledge of the Father. It needs to be extended through a knowledge of the Son, of Christ, through a science which derives from our human potential to take hold of ourselves, to receive an impulse which the soul alone can carry, which does not originate in forces of natural inheritance. The human being is there exposed to a realm not immediately subject to clear laws and causes. He gains access to its laws through the spirit; then, as in the ancient Mysteries, two domains become apparent: the Father-kingdom of nature and the realm of the Spirit; and through the Son, the Christ, we are borne from the natural to the spiritual realm ...

All the questions which can arise when we contemplate the Last Supper really derive from this single question: How can we grasp what takes place in the transubstantiation so as to reconcile it both with the working of the Father within evolution and the working of the Spirit within the laws of nature? The trivial question of miracles is not of importance here, but rather the quite different question of the sacraments ... What we need to consider is that the realm of the Father and the realm of the Spirit are actually active in the world; and between these two stands the Son, who works within the human realm to lift up the kingdom of nature into the domain of Spirit.

The two-thousand-year struggle

Traditional Christianity is a two-thousand-year struggle to come to terms with the Mystery of the 'turning-point' of evolution. The divine Son had come to help each and every human being gain access to the Holy—and healing—Spirit, in order to begin the process of the endless transformation of natural necessity into freedom. This gospel is so 'unbelievable' that at first it could hardly be understood at all.

That is why people were told that they should simply 'believe' in it. But how can one possibly just 'believe' in something that needs to be achieved through freedom? And we must ask what it was that people believed: that Christ worked in the world in a way not dissimilar to the Father? Or did some people, here and there, have an inkling that the working of the Son implied a *reversal* and transformation of the Father's influence into a quest for human freedom?

In such ways we can gain a clearer understanding of the traditional Christianity of 'belief'. Rudolf Steiner's science of the spirit never aims to criticize the past, but to understand its evolutionary necessity. (Such necessity, though, applies only to what has been!) The intervention of the cosmic Son in the life of the earth signifies, as I have said, the beginning of a radical *turning-point* in evolution. The Mystery of Golgotha makes human freedom possible. But to make this freedom reality—to redeem and spiritualize the Father-world of stones, plants, animals, so that ultimately the earth will have been transformed into a 'new earth'—will take all of the second half of evolution. Even today we are still only at the very beginning. Since Christ's Deed at the Mystery of Golgotha, each human being has the potential to take part in this transformation; but he can only actively engage in it by first grasping it as clearly as possible through *thinking*. To grasp freedom requires independent thought. This in turn means that Christ could not draw on the human powers of thinking which already existed, but that He had also to create the possibility for them to unfold. The Christianity of past ages is characterized, therefore, by the fact that Christ worked in the depths of human beings to continually strengthen their faculties of thinking. Only in our own time are people beginning to be able to understand the significance of the fact that evolution ruled by the Father can be transformed by exercising freedom. Thanks to the Christ Event and the continuing working of Christ, the human being has been endowed with all that he needs to transform natural necessity into a new, spiritual Creation perceived through thinking.

The spiritual science of Rudolf Steiner, therefore, represents the beginning of a Christianity based upon ever-increasing *knowledge* and clarity of thinking.

If we now turn our attention to the Christ Event itself, we need to distinguish clearly between the human Christ-bearer Jesus of Nazareth and the Christ Being Himself, the cosmic Son of the divine Father.

Jesus of Nazareth — the embodied religion of humanity

Jesus of Nazareth was a human being who embodied within himself all the many religious paths of humanity. Rudolf Steiner tells us that the individuality of Zarathustra is the one who united in his twelfth year with the Buddha stream, described in the Gospel of St. Luke. The Zarathustra and the Buddha streams were the two central religious tendencies in pre-Christian humanity. The religion of Zarathustra is linked with the tree of knowledge: that is, with human beings' earthly experience, with the Fall of Man, with the continuous cycles of reincarnation. The Buddha religion, on the other hand, is linked with the tree of life: that is, with an aspect of humanity which had remained divinely unsullied, which resided in a state of paradise within the spirituality of the higher ego. This unsullied soul of humanity incarnated for the first time in the Nathan Jesus of St. Luke. It was with this Jesus that the Buddha spiritually united himself. The trees of life and knowledge must be re-united on earth, just as they once were in paradise. Rudolf Steiner speaks of this in his lecture of 19 September 1909 (GA 114):

Thus we see the real and living conjunction of Buddhism with Zarathustrianism. The body in which dwelt the evolved ego-soul of Zarathustra was able to receive and unite itself with what had come about when the astral body of the Nathan Jesus was taken up by the Nirmanakaya Buddha. So we see ripening in Jesus of Nazareth an individuality who bears within himself the ego-being of Zarathustra; who is, at the same time, permeated with the radiant spirit of the rejuvenated Nirmanakaya Buddha. In the soul of Jesus of Nazareth we see this living confluence of Buddhism with Zarathustrianism. Since Joseph of the Nathan line also soon died, the Zarathustra child was in reality an orphan; he felt himself orphaned because his physical descent was not in accord with his real nature. His spirit was that of the reborn Zarathustra. His body descended from his father Joseph, from the line of Nathan—which is how the outer world perceived him. Luke describes this to us in exact terms, and we must take his words literally: '... being (as was supposed) the son of Joseph...'(Luke 3,23).

Zarathustra had sacrificed his etheric body to Moses, so that the cultural stream of Judaism could be founded. He had bequeathed his astral body to Hermes, to enable him to found Egyptian culture. All these partial sacrifices culminated in the sacrifice of his ego, to make way for the Christ Being Himself. I can only give a brief overview here of what Rudolf Steiner described in his lecture cycles on the Matthew and Luke Gospels (GA 123 and 114). At the point where these two converge, Jesus of Nazareth becomes, in his twelfth year, the united embodiment of all humanity's divergent paths of search for divine redemption.

In his lectures on *The Fifth Gospel*, Rudolf Steiner describes how Jesus of Nazareth acquainted himself, between his twelfth and thirtieth year, with Judaism, Paganism and the Essenes. The hopeless, headlong descent of humanity created in him a pain of untold depths, which was transmuted into the highest power of love and sacrifice. In this real and spiritual way, all religious streams converge in the Christ Event. Jesus of Nazareth is the embodiment of humanity's experience of the Fall, and its longing to be redeemed. The future Christ-bearer represents all of us, because into him stream all the questions and strivings of human beings seeking divine redemption.

Because of this, it was possible for the Christ Being, the Being of love, to enter and fill this chalice of humanity, and for the Christ Impulse to pass for three years through the needle's eye of the physical body of Jesus of Nazareth, fulfilling the mystical fact of the Mystery of Golgotha and entering into the physical body of the whole earth.

'Adam's sin' — not a sin at all

The descent into matter, the 'fall into a sundered existence' (for the word sin* is etymologically connected with 'sundering') was necessary. Only by connecting more and more fully with matter could human beings develop individuality. A phrase from scholastic philosophy—*materia principium individuationis*—states that matter is the principle of individualisation. It was a great misunderstanding, a false moralising, to represent the Fall as 'sin', as something morally wrong, and to imply that it would have been better if it had not occurred. Such a point of view negates our whole evolution. The Fall is the pre-requisite for individuality and independence; it gives us the potential for individual knowledge of good and evil. It therefore also enables us to choose to *do* either good or evil.

In itself, then, the Fall is neither 'good' nor 'bad'; it is the precondition for the potential for both. To despise it would be the same as despising freedom. The great myths

---

* The German for the 'Fall of Man' or original sin is '*Sündenfall*' or 'Fall of Sin'. (Transl.)

of all cultures tell of this Mystery of the sundering, dis-
membering and fragmenting of humanity through the
deepening involvement with matter. The bodies of Osiris
and Dionysus were both dismembered; every person
today is like a separate atom of the original unity of mankind.

The first half of evolution—the descent—served to create
the *egoism* of separate, individual identity. In the second
half—the ascent, the redemption—the power of love will
serve to re-unite all people with one another; individuality
will not be lost in this process, but will find its ultimate
fulfillment. Through this re-integration the 'spirit-body of
Christ' will be formed, in which every human being will be
a member. Thus will humanity be redeemed. It was to make
this possible that Christ entered the realm of earth.

The nature of the Fall was characterized by Rudolf Steiner
in the following way in the lecture *How do I find the Christ?*
(16 October 1918, GA 182):

> In the course of evolution, the human soul came to
> associate itself more intimately with the physical world
> than was beneficial. In other words, matter came to exert
> an ever stronger, more forceful influence on people.
> Original sin came about because the 'fallen' human being
> experienced a spirituality that was very much under the
> sway of the power of natural necessity. He became, in his
> thinking, feeling and will-impulses, ever more dependent
> on his physical nature, ever more focused on his physical
> sense-perceptions.

The lecture continues by describing the nature of
redemption: through his working in the earthly realm,
Christ renders the human soul ever more closely related to
the spirit. He transforms all the forces of the earth in such a
way that they are no longer compelling. We can, to the
degree to which we unite ourselves inwardly with Christ,
share in this overcoming of earthly forces. We do not have

to do this, but we can. Freedom consists in overcoming natural necessity through one's own powers.

In creative and active thinking, for example, the living, physiological forces are held at bay and replaced by free thought itself (cf. Rudolf Steiner's *The Philosophy of Freedom*, beginning of chapter 9). When we really call upon our freedom, when we find the moral courage to 'believe' firmly in the possibility of making headway against the natural necessity holding sway in our physical body, then we may continually astonish ourselves that we succeed, that it is really possible: 'All insufficiency here finds completion' (Goethe). We can really experience that our soul becomes as related to spirit, thanks to the deed of love of the Christ Being, as it had to become related to the body through the Fall. The soul's spirit-relatedness is the experience of freedom. Natural necessity is transformed into liberated activity. This occurs initially in our thinking; but through thinking it streams into our will. Thus can the human being experience redemption through the Christ.

The Mystery of Golgotha—the redemption of earth and humanity

What is the real meaning of the Mystery of Golgotha? What actually happened as a result of the death and resurrection of Christ? We can distinguish two aspects, characterized by Rudolf Steiner as a Mystery of the blood and a Mystery of the body. The blood of the Redeemer, dying upon the cross, flowed from His wounds and soaked into the earth, overcoming the egotism in human blood. This egotism was purified and cleansed by the power of love, so that the blood was etherealised. A shining, ethereal aura of love encircled the whole earth.

Since the 'turning-point of time', every human being—whether he knows it or not—lives within this powerful ethereal aura of love. We return repeatedly to earth to learn to live consciously within it. We can see the Mystery of Golgotha as the ecological 'archetypal phenomenon' in the Goethean sense. Through His death and resurrection, the Being of love shows us how we should relate to the earth and the whole physical world.

Christ says of the earth: 'This is my body'. This expresses His commitment of love towards the earth, His will to permeate and redeem it. When human beings begin to perceive the earth's ethereal aura, they will also perceive Christ within this aura, in ethereal form, as the Lord of Karma. Rudolf Steiner speaks of this in the lecture of 2 December 1911 (GA 130), where he describes how people will begin to perceive, in dream-like imaginations, the karmic balancing of their deeds:

I have spoken of a kind of perception of karma; as humanity develops, people will begin, here and there, to have a direct perception of the ethereal Christ in the form in which He dwells on the astral plane. This is a true vision of Christ—not in physical embodiment, but as He appears on earth to newly awakening human faculties; as Protector and Counsellor to people who seek help or comfort in the loneliness of their lives. Times will come in which people feeling downcast and wretched will find the help offered by others to be of ever dwindling worth and significance. The forces of human individuality and independent existence will become ever more pronounced; it will be less and less possible for one person to have a direct and healing influence on the soul of another. But instead, the Great Counsellor will appear here and there in ethereal form...

In contrast to the suffering Christ of Golgotha, Christ appears on earth in the form of Judge, as Christ Triumphant, as Lord of Karma; as such He appears in a form that was already intuited by those who painted the Christ of the Last Judgement ... This actually begins in the twentieth century and continues to the end of earth-existence. The judgement—in other words, the ordering of karma—begins now in the twentieth century.

Alongside this Mystery of the blood at the death of Christ, the Mystery of the body takes place through the entomb-ment and resurrection. The material substance of the body is taken into the earth through a fissure caused by an earthquake. The earth truly 'quakes' and rejoices to receive the communion of the body as token of its redemption.

The science of the spirit sees in the Mystery of Golgotha a complete correspondence between moral deed and natural phenomenon. Nature and morality here become united. Christ's moral Deed is at the same time a Deed which recreates and transforms nature.

During the first half of evolution, these two realms gra-dually separated from one another in order to make human freedom possible. Because our morality or immorality does not directly, simultaneously nourish or ruin nature, we can feel ourselves free. ('Thoughts are duty-free'.)

But all matter longs to be freed from its exile in fixed and rigid forms, and to dissolve back into the cosmos to serve as the foundation for new cosmic creations. For the sake of humanity, infinite numbers of nature beings have made the sacrifice of allowing themselves to be banished in rigid forms. They have done this to enable human beings to *perceive*. To perceive the world is the precondition for thinking it; this task and gift of freedom through thinking is an untold, irreplaceable blessing!

Our actual physical body is a supersensible structure of forces. The matter which makes it visible is really only a material 'filling'. A magnetic field can also not be seen unless we make it visible with, say, iron filings. Rudolf Steiner termed the archetypal form-structure of the human body the 'phantom'. This phantom arose from the grave, and through Christ's Deed its formative forces were restored. For as a result of laws specific to matter, the supersensible forms and forces had increasingly declined and become distorted. If they had not been redeemed, the human being would eventually have become unable to structure a bodily form at birth that was appropriate to his humanity.

The Mystery of the resurrected body—the phantom—is the Mystery of all form and metamorphosis. It incorporates the whole task of human thinking, whose content is given through material substance and by the world of perceptible forms. 'The Word became flesh' means: the cosmic Word becomes visible to us through sense-perception, so that we have the possibility of fulfilling the resurrection of the body through creative thinking. The earth as body of the Logos is transformed into the spiritual body of the human being through thinking. The Word become flesh shares in the resurrection of the flesh and through the human love of thinking becomes Word once more.

The exile of all creation in perceptible forms is portrayed in folktales as 'enchantment'. All creation longs to be redeemed from transience. We should therefore be glad that the earth is in the process of dissolution. This process should of course not come about too quickly and too soon, but also not too slowly and too late. We should be glad that 'Heaven and Earth shall pass away'. Every creature and being rejoices that it will one day shed the transitory form it assumed for the sake of mankind, when the cosmic sacrifice of love culminates in human freedom.

Through human thinking all things can be resurrected within the human spirit. To be incorporated into humanity in this way fulfills the longing of all creation, just as to be permeated by Christ fulfills humanity's longing. The new creation which continually resurrects in human thinking out of the grave of earth, is the living, spiritual 'phantom', the actual spirit-being of all things. The phantom body-nature of the resurrected Being of love contains all formative forces and structures of earth evolution, and offers mankind the infinite quest of achieving freedom through intuitive thinking.

Since the Christ Event, then, a double Christ-aura encircles the earth as the essence of the Christ *Impulse*. One aura is His ethereal aura of love, containing all possible Intuitions of love accessible to human beings. The moral Imagination of Christ's love is cosmic and all-encompassing. Through the all-encompassing Imagination of his love, He has grasped the fulfilled redemption of earth and humanity. All our potential moral Intuitions are contained therein.

The second aura is the phantom-aura, containing all possible Intuitions of knowledge and understanding. These two auras correspond to the two sections of Rudolf Steiner's *Philosophy of Freedom*. The first section deals with cognitive Intuitions, in which the pure laws underlying all things are understood as the Logos-content of the 'ideational monism' of the world. The second section is concerned with the moral Intuitions which enable us to learn, in a loving way, to take karma seriously—so that all people can one day be re-incorporated into each other, and so that the spirit body of Christ can be formed into the supersensible, unified organism of humanity; and so that within the human being, all creatures can be resurrected.

Fundamental tenets of Christianity

We can only really understand the most important and fundamental doctrines of Christianity if we look upon the Christ Mystery as the turning-point of evolution. One of these fundamental tenets says: The Father sends the Son; the Father *and the Son* (filioque) send the Holy Spirit. If we interpret this in terms of *The Philosophy of Freedom*, the phrase 'The Father sends the Son' means that natural necessity finds its fulfillment in freedom. Natural necessity has provided the being of freedom—the human being—with both the overall conditions for seeking freedom, and the ultimate task of achieving it. Human freedom is experienced when thinking permeates what is naturally given—what can be perceived—so that it is transformed into the thought-essence of the being of freedom himself.

The Father world is the physical and mineral realm, the world of natural necessity and of all that can be perceived. The Father, the highest divinity, spiritually permeates the mineral foundations of existence. In ancient languages there is a single word to designate both the divine Father and the dead mineral realm: Latin and Greek speak of 'pater / petra' (father / stone); Hebrew has 'av' (father) and 'even' (stone). The Father who permeates the dead, mineral world, sends the Son; and thus natural necessity opens itself to the being of freedom. The Father *sends* the Son, wishes to send Him: natural necessity is not there to hinder freedom but to make it possible. All of Creation looks to, and longs for, the being of freedom.

The reason we live in a Father-world of natural necessity is that this Word-become-flesh is waiting for us to achieve freedom by means of it. We should understand that our task consists in allowing the Word-become-flesh to be resurrected once more through our thinking Intuition. Natural necessity (the 'flesh') thus resurrects into the word-consciousness of human thinking. Because the Holy Spirit—that is, the experience of individual freedom through thinking—is sent not only by the Father but *also by the Son*, the human being is not merely a passive reflection of the Father Spirit; through the Son he becomes a renewed and transformed being of spirit. This spirit nature is itself divine and creative—as we can hear in Christ's words in the St. John Gospel: 'Ye are gods' (John, 10, 34).

Another important doctrine of Christianity can be found in the words (John, 14, 12): 'He that believeth on me, the works that I do shall he do also; and greater works than these shall he do; because I go unto my Father.' This has always baffled theologians. But its full meaning and significance becomes clear in the present context. Christ speaks this during his words of farewell; He has not yet gone through the experience of death, of 'going to the Father'. The 'lesser works' of evolution took place before the turning-point of time which is about to take place. They derived from the human spirit's fear and incapacity in the face of the physical and material world. People considered the earth, the realm of matter, as a place of 'sin'—that is, a place where human beings had fallen and failed; they longed simply to depart from it and return to the realm of spirit.

Christ's decision to 'go to the Father' is the decision to go through death. Rudolf Steiner tells us, in his lectures *The Gospel of St. John in Relation to the Other Gospels*, given in Kassel in 1909 (GA 112), that the occult meaning of 'the Father' is death. It is in the dead mineral realm that the Father is to be found. Christ unites Himself with the physical body of the earth and so inaugurates the 'greater works' of evolution. Since Christ's death, human beings no longer desire to flee the earth, they are no longer afraid of matter. The *opus magnum* begins, the 'great work' of matter's transformation through the human spirit. Christianity is the love of spirit for matter. This love transfigures and renders human the whole of creation.

The radical difference of the Christian trinity

The radical departure from the divine trinity in pre-Christian religions which the Christian trinity represents, can only be understood through a true experience of human freedom. The world of the Father is what provides the outer conditions for freedom; the working of the Son endows the human being with an inner capacity for freedom. There is no love greater than that which enables the loved one to attain spiritual autonomy—which is what freedom is. Each human soul bears within itself, thanks to the workings of Christ, the potential and capacity for freedom. But potential still needs to be realized. The distinction, drawn clearly by the schools of Aristotle and Aquinas, between capacity and fulfillment, is of great importance.

Christ cannot endow us with freedom, He cannot make us free. Freedom is a *human* experience only by virtue of the fact that it arises as an intuitional act of creativity in the human being himself, possible only through his own active thinking. Only the outer *conditions* for freedom can be provided. That is why a third aspect is needed: an experience of the Holy Spirit. The difference between soul and spirit is so enormous and decisive—in just the same way as is the distinction between potential and realization—that Christ says to the Apostles (John, 16, 7): 'It is expedient for you that I go away: for if I go not away, the Comforter (the Holy Spirit) will not come unto you [and be in you]'. It is not enough for the human being to remain passive and wait for all to be given him through the grace of Christ. All passivity of soul must end, must be conquered and superseded by activity of the spirit. A distinction must be made between an experience of Christ and an experience of the Holy Spirit: they are not one and the same.

Christ's words at this point mean that passivity and activity are incompatible. An experience of the Holy Spirit supersedes all guidance from without. This experience is accessible to anyone who takes hold of the capacity for freedom dwelling in his soul, and realizes the freedom of the spirit through active, creative thinking. Capacity for freedom (the human being as soul) arises from the workings of the Son; the fulfillment of freedom (the human being as spirit) is an experience of the Holy Spirit.

To sum up once more: the Father realm establishes the

overall outer conditions for freedom to unfold. The workings of the Son endow the soul with the inner capacity and potential for freedom. In the experience of the Holy Spirit, freedom is realized and fulfilled. We can therefore understand the threefold structure of existence—body, soul and spirit, as Rudolf Steiner described it in his book *Theosophy*—out of an experience of human freedom. The aim of all evolution is contained here: that humanity attains the tenth, divine hierarchy, the 'hierarchy of freedom' (cf. GA 110, the lecture of 18 April 1909). The hierarchies cannot know the specifically *human* form of freedom, for they do not have any experience of overcoming and transforming the dead, mineral realm.

This trinity of the human cosmos can also be derived from a direct experience of freedom itself.

Freedom can, by its very nature, be either neglected or fulfilled: it is the human being's prerogative to choose between these two. It *must* remain possible for us to fail to realize freedom; then the world of the Father reasserts itself—the realm of unfree necessity. The human being must always have the free choice to follow a course which leads him to be subsumed once more by natural necessity, thus losing himself as a free being. That is why the Father-realm must be there.

For the other attribute of freedom, the fact that it can be achieved, each one of us must thank the workings of the Son. In the choice between realizing and failing to realize freedom, we experience within ourselves the Holy Spirit: either as holy, when freedom is fulfilled, or unholy when the opportunity for it is missed.

This Spirit is 'holy' in the sense that there can be no access to it from without. Sinning against the Holy Spirit, against one's own freedom, cannot be 'forgiven' from without. Whoever 'sins' against his own spirit—whoever, in other words, sunders himself from his spirit's free, creative activity by subjecting himself to the dominion of the physical world—can only want it and regain it once more through his own means. The great sins against freedom are ones of omission. Emphasis on the committing of sins belongs to an early stage of human evolution, before freedom became possible.

The Being of love came to transform the negative morality of 'Thou shalt not' into a positive one of 'You can, you may, you have the will'. Christ did not come to ordain or forbid but to offer freedom to each one of us. This offer, though, was initially taken as a command: 'A new commandment I give unto you, That ye love one another; as I have loved you, that ye also love me' (John, 13, 34). The Greek word translated here as command is ἐντολή (entolé). It is a variant of the word τέλος (telos, aim) and derives from a root-verb form which expresses the indwelling force and intentionality of a being—particularly the forces of growth and metamorphosis in the realm of plants. Love cannot be a 'command', for it arises only out of freedom. Christ's words actually mean: I come to tell you in what way man can enter into (εv = in) the realization and fulfilment of his being: through love. Only love, which depends upon freedom, can enable the human being to attain his aim, his perfection. Christ speaks of a *new* 'command', but the command to love is not new; what is new is the offer of love as the inexhaustible task of freedom.

The science of the spirit provides us with the necessary basis for understanding human freedom as an expression of divine *love*. If the divine, cosmic Father had also retained absolute sway over the human being, if we were still ruled and influenced by the direct workings of the Father-realm, human freedom would be impossible. For this reason the Father relinquished omnipotence over the human soul, sharing his power with Ahriman. In a similar way, the Holy Spirit renounced omniscience, intentionally dispensing with foreknowledge of the human being's deeds of thinking, feeling and willing. Instead the Holy Spirit shares its wisdom with Lucifer. In the human realm, and for the sake of humanity, the Father rendered himself 'feeble and powerless' and the Holy Spirit became 'unknowing and foolish'. That is why the human being can himself freely determine what takes place within himself.

Christ, the Being of love, reveals Himself in divine powerlessness and foolishness—for to love means to renounce power and control over another, to give up 'knowing what's best' for another. The Being of love, the Christ Being, is not a divine power which overpowers us and determines us from without, nor one which claims foreknowledge of our intentions. Christ's love is an absolute and pure love which desires human beings to be free. Christ wants us to be free. His will is only done by those who practise and exercise freedom.

2
THE HISTORY OF 'ALL-TOO-HUMAN' CHRISTIANITY

Let us now turn our attention to the history of Christianity. We are justified in calling this 'Petrine-Christianity'. In the two thousand years which have elapsed since the Mystery of Golgotha, humanity has had to sink still deeper into materialism. If Christ had delayed His coming to the 'twelfth' instead of the 'eleventh hour', human beings would no longer have had the remotest possibility of grasping this Mystery. Christ in fact said to Peter: 'Follow me' (John, 21, 19). It was the task of Petrine-Christianity to follow directly from the Christ Event.

Christ said of John, His spiritual pupil, that he must wait until He should come again. Picking up the thread of our observations up to this point, we can say that Petrine-Christianity was a Christianity of the soul. Christ wishes, initially, to build His 'church' on the Petrine-Rock; each church, as such, is still an expression of the group-soul, not yet of independent, spiritual individuality. Through the science of the spirit we can have an experience of the Second Coming of Christ, which will now gradually enable us to gain access to a Christianity of the spirit. Christ Himself gave Peter his name: after 'petra', stone or rock. It is into the dead, mineral realm—that is, into materialism—that humanity has descended most deeply since that time.

The Mystery of Golgotha took place at the penultimate hour before humanity descended into the deepest abyss of materialism. Christ Himself accompanied humanity's 'journey to the Father' right down to its ultimate consequence. Part and parcel of this process was the ever deepening materialism, through the centuries, of

Christianity itself. Let us look now at the course of its history through just some of its decisive events and phenomena.

In the fourth century, as a result of the influence of Constantine, Christianity was declared a state religion. That was the point at which it began to be a force in earthly affairs. We know how decisive this earthly power became for the Catholic Church in subsequent centuries. I have always thought, when considering this turn of events, of Christ's words: 'My kingdom is not of this world' (John, 18, 36). Christ came to transform the earthly world into a spiritual one, but in the fourth century His intention was turned upon its head. The Christianity which then began could, in many ways, be summed up by the phrase: 'My kingdom *is* of this world'.

This Christianity is our own past, the heritage of all of us. Whoever properly understands the science of the spirit will not harbour any ill-will towards this past. Through Rudolf Steiner's science of the spirit we can learn to accept as self-evident that the church had gradually to lose every vestige of the treasures of spiritual knowledge. It is only because less and less is forthcoming from this source, that each one of us has the possibility to seek and find the spirit once more out of individual freedom. Anyone who still looks towards the church for spiritual sustenance and guidance, is seeking it from without, and thus evading his own, individual, free striving.

A further aspect of the history of this Petrine-Christianity is described by Rudolf Steiner as the Mass becoming exoteric (cf., for example, GA 237, the lecture of 11 July 1924). Throughout the history of humanity people had always been forbidden to take part in the Mysteries in an ordinary everyday frame of mind. Only those were admitted who had passed through an inner transformation. The right inner mood was necessary. Inner change was requisite for sharing in the change celebrated in the ritual. The Mass was originally a synthesis of the deepest Mystery secrets; but as a result of the fact that all were now admitted to its whole ritual sequence, the inner requirements were no longer really taken seriously.

Another important historical event took place in the year 869, at the Eighth Ecumenical Council in Constantinople, when, as Rudolf Steiner said many times, the spirit was 'abolished'. The Trichotomy—an awareness that the human being consists of body, soul *and* spirit—was lost. From that point onwards, the human being was considered to have only a body and soul, although the latter was still thought to possess some spiritual characteristics. It is only a small step from this idea to the Darwinian belief that the human being is a higher animal. 'Animal', deriving from the Latin, in fact means 'soul-being' (*anima* = soul). The science of the second half of the last century is nothing other than the executor of the legacy of the Eighth Ecumenical Council. Any con- sciousness of the eternal individuality, the spirit-ego of each person, became more and more veiled in darkness.

The dispute over the Last Supper

The dispute and struggle over the Last Supper is a very important aspect of the evolution of traditional Christianity. Rudolf Steiner observes that whenever people begin to argue about something, it is always a sign that an under- lying context is no longer understood. In earlier centuries, Christians were still able to have a deep belief in, and an intuitive connection with, the transubstantiation. Later on people began to dispute whether bread and wine were really the body and blood of Christ, or whether the con- nection was just a symbolic one. I have already spoken of the nature of Christian transformation, in its deepest and most comprehensive sense, as the metamorphosis, through the human being, of natural necessity into the realm of freedom.

We invariably stop short of this metamorphosis when-ever we experience the material, visible world as more substantial and real than the world of spirit. We then feel ourselves, our spirit, to be derived from and influenced by the sense-perceptible world. In these circumstances we stop short also of Christ. But each time that we manage to have an inward experience of the realm of spirit by imbu-ing our concept of it with intuitive and active thinking—each time that we manage to experience it in such a real, substantial, living way that we are assured that the spirit is more deep-rooted and 'substantial' than matter—then we truly transubstantiate the world. The essence of Chris-tianity lies in the creative force of the thinking human spirit, which experiences the spirit as more substantial than so-called matter. Within and through the human being is experienced the full reality, the *primum mobile*, of the realm of spirit.

But it is not enough just to assert that the spirit, of itself, is more substantial than matter. The necessary transformation can only come about through our own creative activity, our own actual experience. In *The Philosophy of Freedom*, Rudolf Steiner describes this transubstantiation of the world through human thinking. By becoming aware that the sense-perceptible realm offers nothing of 'substance', the human being forms concepts through his thinking which create spiritual substance. This is, in the highest sense, the Christian transubstantiation of the world.

The ritual transformation which takes place through the priest as representative should not be thought to replace the task of inner transformation which each individual has to realize in his own inner experience of the Holy Spirit. Christ's words: 'This do in remembrance of me' mean that the Christian ritual should 'remind' human beings of the task that evolution presents them with. 'This do in remembrance of the I' one could say; so as to be reminded, in other words, that the ultimate aim of evolution is egohood—the fulfilled power of the human spirit. In his lecture of 13 October 1911 (GA 131), Rudolf Steiner says:

As long as people still knew that the Last Supper was a true manifestation and living testimony of the fact that matter is not matter alone; as long as they still knew that ritual ceremonies exist by means of which matter can be imbued with spirit—and that matter is thus permeated by Christ, as occurred at the Last Supper—then this event was still accepted for what it was, without debate or conflict ... The Last Supper gave those who wished to approach the Christ, but could not follow an esoteric path, the means to do so; in the Last Supper they were able to unite themselves truly with Christ ... And just as the less evolved Christian could seek Christ through the Last Supper, so the more evolved Christian, who comes to know the figure of Christ by means of the new science of the spirit, can already lift himself in spirit to what in future times should become once more an exoteric path for human beings. This will bring an influx of strength that should broaden and deepen the Christ Impulse for humanity. But when this happens, all rituals and ceremonies will also change: what previously took place through the attributes(?)* of bread and wine, will in future be replaced by a spiritual Last Supper. But the import of the Last Supper and the Communion will still remain. What is needed is for certain inner thoughts, inner feelings and intuitions—which flow through us in response to what we hear within our spiritual scientific movement—to permeate and spiritualize our inward life in just as solemn and ceremonious a way as the Last Supper, in the best sense of inner Christian evolution, permeated the human soul with Christ. When this

---

*This question-mark occurs in the original German. The author is questioning whether this is really the word Steiner intended. It could have been a mistake on the part of the stenographer. (Transl.)

becomes possible—and it will—we will have taken a step further in evolution. And this will be a real testimony to the fact that Christianity is greater than its outer forms … You can only have a true idea of Christianity when you are fully convinced that all churches which profess belief in Christ, as well as all outer forms and thoughts about Christ, are transitory; but that the Christ Thought, in ever new forms, will enter in the future into the hearts and souls of human beings, however little evidence there may be of this at the present time.

I have a memory of myself as a very young child, kneeling in the church next to my mother during Mass; I can still hear how enormously loud the silence was during the con-secration of the bread and wine at the altar. I can say from experience that these peasant-folk lived, at such moments, fully in a world of spirit. Christ was a real, living presence for them. Such moments were a source of spiritual strength which carried these people through a life that was often hard; a source which could be experienced without calling on the consciousness soul, and without the insights of a science of the spirit. This was still possible for my mother's generation—but no longer for her son's. I belong to those who either relate to the transubstantiation through think-ing, or for whom it remains unreal. Such people are becoming ever more numerous.

Once the transubstantiation could no longer be experi-enced, people were no longer able to understand what was meant in the New Testament—to give just one important example—by the 'end of the world'. People started to think that this referred to an actual, physical end of all things. But the early Christians meant something quite different: that the Father-world had relinquished its dominance through the divine Son entering the earthly realm. The Father-world was no longer the sole cause of everything; instead, it now provided the conditions out of which freedom could

evolve. Natural necessity had surrendered its all-deter-
mining role: that is the real meaning of 'the end of the
world'. Henceforth, nature *can* still exert a dominant
influence on the human being, but does not *have* to.

It is only by looking at things in this way that we come
close to the ideas people had in the first centuries after
Christ. Their view of things showed them that they
should not rely on any power other than the power of
their own consciousness to gain access to the thoughts
which led them to the divine. People were drawn
towards the realm of spirit. What, therefore, could be said
to them? The following could be said: Previously the
earth was so mighty that it furnished you with your idea
of the divine. But that has ended. The earth no longer
opens the way to the divine. Now you must, instead, find
your way to the Logos and the creative principle through
your own self. Until now you have really worshipped the
creative principle that was active before the earth was
formed (and which formed it). Now you should honour
the creative power within the earthly realm. But you can
only do this through the strength of your ego, of your
spirit.

This was expressed by the early Christians saying that
'The end of the world is nigh'. They meant the end of that
world which provided human beings with knowledge
without the need for them to work consciously to attain it.
This 'end of the world' represents a deep truth; until then,
the human being was a son of earth and gave himself up to
earthly forces. He relied on the knowledge given to him
through his blood. This had ended. The heavenly realms
descended; the earthly realms' power waned. The human
being can no longer be a son of the earth. He must now
make himself into a companion of the Being of spirit who
descended to earth from spiritual realms—the Logos, the
Christ. (Lecture by Rudolf Steiner, 3 June, 1921, GA 204.)

Another very important characteristic of traditional Christianity is the loss of any awareness of reincarnation and karma. Rudolf Steiner emphasizes that the Christian cultures of the West actually had the task of allowing this awareness to fade for a while (cf., for example, the lecture of 1 January 1919, GA 187). This can be said, in fact, to have been the central task of Petrine-Christianity itself. The fading of knowledge of reincarnation and karma also led to the loss of the idea of pre-existence. The Aristotelian teaching was adopted, which says that the human being is only divinely created at the point of conception.

Plato still very much affirmed the idea of pre-existence. Aristotle is the first great western thinker unable to imagine the human being separate from his physical body; this body is, for him, an essential aspect of his experience of himself. Aristotle even regards human 'immortality' as an eternal backward glance to one's own cast-off physical body. The Christian idea of immortality spoke very strongly to human egotism. Everyone, of course, would be happy to continue their existence after death. In response to this desire, the 'immortality of the soul' was continually spoken of.

But Rudolf Steiner emphasizes that it is equally important to think in terms of the 'unborn-hood' of the human being: the human spirit itself is neither born nor dies. The knowledge that we enter the physical world from a world of spirit, with a task and mission to balance the disharmony or deficit from our previous earthly lives, cannot be an idea that flatters our egotism. Instead it calls upon our sense of moral responsibility and earnest endeavour.

But what is the real significance of the fact that people lost all awareness of reincarnation and karma? The Mystery of the higher ego—the true spirit of the human being that continues from one life to the next—was, as a result, shrouded in darkness. People could no longer understand that their daily lives were embedded in karmic forces; and that all that they had to endure was freely, consciously chosen and planned by their higher ego before birth, in communion with the spiritual hierarchies. In the lecture I have already quoted from (11 September 1924, GA 346), Rudolf Steiner describes the inseparable unity of the Christian Mystery of transubstantiation with the Mystery of karma. The loss of understanding for one was accompanied, inevitably, by the loss of understanding for the other.

> Let us look for a moment at any human action. We can view it from two different angles: either as the result of a person's heredity, through father, mother, grandfather, grandmother, etc.; or also as the result of forces which derive from previous earthly lives. This is a quite different realm, which is why it cannot be understood in ordinary scientific—or 'Father-knowledge'—terms.
>
> Now there are two things which appear different, but are actually essentially the same. The first is the way karma or destiny evolves as the result of past earthly lives: this is certainly no visible, natural law, but is still a law nevertheless. We perceive the second when we look at the altar and realize that the transubstantiation is also not outwardly visible, but that it takes place as spiritual reality within physical substance. We can bring these two things together: the way in which karma works, and the way in which the transubstantiation occurs. Whoever understands the first will also be able to understand the second.

An unbridgeable chasm came to be imagined between the human and the divine, because of the idea that we live only once. The way we now live and die, at our present stage of evolution, is surely 'all too human' for us to avoid seeing all our imperfections. The primal disparity between God and Man became ever more pronounced. God's transcendence—the quite other nature of the divine—was emphasized more and more.

From the point of view of reincarnation, in contrast, each person has the fundamental potential to evolve towards his divine nature. Each person has the opportunity to develop through many lives, to accumulate the qualities which were brought to visible human perfection in the Christ Being. The so-called 'miracles' of Christ are spoken of, in the Gospel of St. John, as 'signs'. Through them, Christ shows us what each person is capable of, and is called upon to develop in the course of his evolution.

The Being of love did not come to show humanity by His deeds what it is *not* capable of attaining. That was, in fact, how the devil tempted Christ at the very beginning, by saying: Show human beings your divine, superhuman abilities, transform stone into bread, cast yourself down from the pinnacle of the temple ... Christ's response was His free decision to renounce everything that was beyond the bounds of human possibility, to limit Himself to what lies within the capacities of human evolution. We can interpret the 'miracles' in a quite different light when we view them from the perspective of reincarnation: Christ's deeds show what it is possible for us to attain. He Himself shows us what we *can* become in the course of our evolution. We must on no account judge human nature according to our present 'fallen' state. The perfection of our human nature is given to us, so far, only in Christ. Christ is not 'beyond' us; we are, rather, at the present stage of our evolution, still not nearly 'human' enough.

It has often been asserted that awareness of reincarnation has always been retained in the East. But this is only half the truth. Inherent in pre-Christian religions is not the idea of reincarnation as such, but rather the 'transmigration of souls' or metempsychosis. The difference between these two ideas is an enormous one, no less significant than that between soul and spirit. Reincarnation is the law which underlies the evolution of the ego, of the human spirit as eternal individuality. Before Christ, human beings had almost no possibility of experiencing the ego in a real sense.

In the fifth lecture of his lecture-cycle *From Jesus to Christ* (GA 131), Rudolf Steiner discusses the pre-Christian struggle for an experience of the ego in ancient Greece, in Buddhism and in ancient Hebrew times. The ancient Greek had a sense of himself as a separate individual, but only thanks to his physical body. After death, in a bodiless state, he felt himself to be only the shadow of a human being. Buddhism, in its original teachings, looks upon the ego as an illusion, from which one should free oneself by departing from the physical plane. Within the Jewish faith there arose a real concept of the ego, but ascribed only to the 'Yahveh' (or 'I am'). Human beings could only partake in this ego-nature through the physical blood-inheritance passed down through the Hebrews—the Yahveh-people— and through their inner experience of the Yahveh laws. Both of these aspects of ego-experience are dictated by the group-soul.

What is quite new, made possible by the Christ Being's descent into the earth, is an absolute experience of the ego that is *simultaneously wholly spiritual and wholly individual*. This experience alone enables us to have a real consciousness of reincarnation. Before this, one could only really speak of the 'transmigration of souls'.

Forgiveness of sins

In the same way, forgiveness of sins could not, in the past, be viewed through the perspective of karma and of the independent, reincarnating ego. The human 'soul' could be cleansed without the individual needing to take full and conscious responsibility for the process. In a similar way, we can forgive children a great deal. Christ sums up the pre-Christian basis for forgiveness with the words: 'Father, forgive them; for they know not what they do' (Luke 23,34).

The important question posed here is this: does it serve evolution if the human being, in all future times, is unaware of what he does? The answer given by the science of the spirit is: Christ came to earth to enable each person to evolve an ever clearer *knowledge* of his actions. Those who accuse Rudolf Steiner's science of the spirit of calling for self-redemption, and thus rendering redemption through Christ superfluous, are labouring under a severe misapprehension.

In the lectures *Christ and the Human Soul* (GA 155), Rudolf Steiner distinguishes between *karmic* and *cosmic* consequences of every human deed. The karmic consequences are those which arise in the inner life of the doer—the changes in his ego and in the threefold organization of his being. The cosmic consequences, on the other hand, are what occurs objectively in the world as a result of human actions and behaviour. Each person can and must balance and harmonize the karmic consequences of his deeds within himself, through exercising freedom. The sin against the Holy Spirit *cannot* be forgiven from without. Inherent in the essence of freedom is that it would be violated by an outside influence.

The objective, 'cosmic' consequences are quite different in this respect. We are capable only of redressing this balance to a very small extent. Rudolf Steiner gives the extreme example of a person who gouges out another person's eyes. If the one who has become blind—who may for example be a farmer—then makes rather a mess of things, the perpetrator of the blinding is unlikely to be able to put this damage right. If we understand the full implications of this, we will realize what is meant when John the Baptist says of the Christ Being: 'Behold the Lamb of God, which taketh away the sin of the world.' (John, 1,29.)

In the Greek it does not say, though, that Christ takes upon Himself the sin of mankind or of the earth; but the sin 'of the cosmos' (κόσμου tou kosmou). I can still clearly remember the joy and inner liberation I experienced when I first read what Rudolf Steiner has to say about this distinction between cosmic and karmic consequences. This passage from the Gospel of St. John then came vividly to mind, and I realized how important it is to carefully weigh up each single word of this text!

Christ takes upon himself the cosmic—that is to say, the objective, outer—consequences of our deeds. If the Being of love were not to continually do this, we would have wrought such damage to the earth that it would by now hardly be habitable by us. What grace that He made of the earth *His* body! The insights of the science of the spirit do not accord the influence of grace less worth; on the contrary, they honour and value it infinitely more highly than would otherwise be the case. Only through this science do we learn of all that the Being of love does for us, all that we receive from Him through grace. The sin of the adulteress (John 8), is engraved by Christ into the earth, into His body.

The Holy Scripture—not so 'holy' any longer

I would like to mention one other significant characteristic of Petrine-Christianity: its relationship to the Holy Scriptures. The Christian Church has had the basic conviction that the New Testament reveals to us all that is to be known of Christ, and that everything which He had to say to mankind is contained within it. We need only bring clearer and clearer understanding to bear upon the ultimate revelations of the New Testament; an understanding which, according to orthodoxy, the Church alone has access and right to.

This point of view manages to exclude the possibility of humanity directly relating to the Christ Being, of coming into contact with Him in a continual and unmediated way.

According to such a teaching, Christ has already said everything that He wanted to, and, moreover, finds access to human beings only through the church.

In the relationship of Christianity to the Holy Scriptures, we can also see the decisive influence of the turning-point of the last few centuries, in which, according to Rudolf Steiner, the fifth cultural epoch began. As late as the eighteenth century, people still related in a deep, feeling way to the Gospels. Christ Himself worked within humanity through these texts—not through reason and understanding, but through the power of faith.

But when, in the last century, people began to adopt historical and scientific standards in researching these texts, our modern faculty of logic and reason could only pull them to pieces. They emerged as historically wholly unreliable documents. Bible criticism has really pulled the carpet from under the feet of the important dogma that the Scriptures are divinely inspired. This dogma could only mean that the Scriptures derived from other than just ordinary human faculties. To say that they are inspired by the Holy Spirit means, after all, that capacities were at work in creating them which are not available to 'normal' people.

Reading Steiner, I have always had the impression that he retrieves this dogma of the divine inspiration of the Scriptures. He tells us that the evangelists were initiates and that they were fully conscious of what they were writing. As well as physical events and facts, the Gospels describe *supersensible* ones, which must be understood with other than the normal, physical organs of perception. I have known a good few professors of theology who were expert at the exegesis of the Scriptures, who knew better than Matthew, Mark and Luke who had copied what from whom, and which discrepancies could be found—for example between these last-mentioned Gospels and that of St. John. Such a professor could, of course, strike out repetitions, correct mistakes and produce an altogether better text!

Let me give just one example to illustrate the relationship many people have to the inspired text of the Gospels: the so-called walking of Christ on the water. Within traditional Christianity we would only have two interpretative possibilities: either He was divine and could do anything, including walking on the water; or the passage is meant symbolically—it is an image intended to express some moral or doctrine.

When we examine both interpretations, neither of them, though, stand up to scrutiny for a moment. The first version ascribes black-magic practices to Christ. If He had actually walked upon the water in a physical sense, this would have violated human freedom—for no one can feel free in the presence of someone who physically walks over water. Christ would not have become truly human if he had defied the fundamental laws, such as gravity, which we are subject to. The other alternative—that this is a metaphorical image—would mean that everything in the Gospels could be interpreted only as symbol. Why, in that case, should we not consider the raising of Lazarus, the resurrection of Christ, or even Christ's very existence as mythical imagery? In fact there are some who have had the courage to follow this train of thought to its logical conclusion, and have declared the whole business to be a nice myth. According to them, certain people just got hold of the idea of a Christ-myth two thousand years ago—in much the same way as Faust sprang up in Goethe's mind. It would be naive, of course, to demand that Goethe tell us exactly when and how all the events he describes actually happened.

Reading Rudolf Steiner's works, I found something quite different, which for me is the sole solution to the dilemma. He tells us that the Apostles had a real, supersensible vision of the *spiritual* Christ Being upon the sea. Both their

perception and what they perceived were absolute realities—but not of a physical, material kind.

The two traditional interpretations have a materialistic
outlook in common. Underlying both is the idea that either
something real occurs, which is of a physical nature (first
interpretation), or nothing of a physical nature occurs, in
which case nothing has actually happened (second interpretation). That is why Rudolf Steiner's science of the spirit
is, in our time, the only way of getting beyond materialism.
According to Rudolf Steiner, modern theology itself has
substantially contributed to this materialism.

I would like, in passing at least, to add a reference to
contemporary New Testament exegesis. In the sequence of
publications entitled *Paths of Research**, volume 522 is called
The Resurrection of Jesus according to the New Testament.†
Contained in this is an essay by Rudolf Pesch, *How Belief
arose in Jesus' Resurrection,*‡ from which I quote the following passage:

> In this situation I worked out an hypothesis on 'how
> belief arose in Jesus' resurrection', which not only dis-
> pensed with debate about the 'empty grave', but also
> with the derivation of belief in the Easter event from an
> unspecifiable occurrence of vision.

Let me translate this for the layman. Two factors which
could play a part in 'belief in the resurrection' are excluded:
firstly, the empty grave—in other words any objective
reality connected with nature, earth and the physical body
of Jesus; secondly, any 'occurrence of vision'—in other
words, any kind of perception of supersensible reality. The
exegete is here thinking in terms of hallucinatory vision,

---

* *Wege der Forschung,* published by the Wissenschaftliche Buchge-
sellschaft.
† *Zur Neutestamentliche Überlieferung von der Auferstehung Jesu,* edited by
Paul Hoffmann (Darmstadt, 1988).
‡ *'Zur Entstehung des Glaubens an die Auferstehung Jesu'.*

which is why he wishes to exclude it as a basis for belief—
but thus also excludes the possibility of any real experience
of the spiritual presence of the Risen One.

If these two factors—natural, physical reality, and the
spiritual and supersensible realm—are excluded, what are
we left with? Only *soul*: in other words, the inner memories
and feelings with which the disciples, after His death,
interpreted the experiences they had had with the man
Jesus during his lifetime. It is simply assumed that their
experiences cannot be much different from those possible
for the average human being of today. Not for a moment is
there any thought that Jesus could be experienced in any
other than the normal way we are used to nowadays.
Human nature, as we know it today, is taken as the absolute
standard, whose characteristics have always remained
constant and will always do so in the future. Contemporary
human beings thus ordain how Jesus must have been in
order to be a real 'human being', instead of trying to learn
from Christ of the mighty transformations which human
nature must still undergo, so as to become wholly 'human'
in the course of our evolution towards divine nature. People
nowadays—the theologian quoted here of course inclu-
ded—are no longer aware that human nature has the
potential to develop organs of perception for supersensible
reality, which can perceive differently—but no less objectively—than we perceive through our physical senses.

We touch here upon a decisive difference between
traditional Christianity and the science of the spirit of
Rudolf Steiner. Steiner attaches fundamental importance to
something which is more or less absent in the tenets of
Christianity: the evolutionary perspective. Not only is
human nature continually evolving, but the way in which
Christ relates to and communicates with us also changes
over the course of time.

Christ Himself said: 'I am with you until the end of the
earth'. He, the Risen One, accompanies us; our repeated

earthly lives give each one of us the possibility of establishing a real connection with Him, and in a constantly
changing way. Of the earth He said: 'This is my body'. His
Ascension to the heavens was in reality a descent into the
earth: for heaven is where Christ is. He *is* the heavens.

From Christ to Jesus — the dear, poor 'God'

If we wish to sum up the history of Christianity, we have to
say that a real understanding of the Christ Being continually dwindled; what remained in the end was only
Jesus—the 'simple man of Nazareth'. Although the word
'Christ' is still used, nothing more is meant by it than the
influence of a human personality.

A similar thing happened to the concept of 'God'. Rudolf
Steiner writes that the modern Christian's idea of God is
only just sufficient to enable him to imagine some kind of
angel-being. Since each person has their own different
guardian angel, everyone also imagines 'God' in a different
way. The divine, therefore, which ought to encompass and
unite all people, in fact only serves to fragment and isolate
them in endless dispute and disagreement. The source of
materialism, deeply rooted in this concept of God, wells up
in the radical divergence and confrontation between people, in the emphasis placed on competition and on asserting
one's individual right to possession at the expense of others.
But it goes further than this: the misinterpretation of, or
blindness towards, the Christ-focused harmony of the
archangels, leads to *Nationalism*. Perversion of the Epoch
Spirit's inspiration gives rise to *cosmic guilt* towards the
Earth Spirit. Rudolf Steiner says:

> We must be fully aware that, in many respects, the
> answer to the question 'Who must bear the blame for the
> materialism of our time?' is: religion. The religious faiths
> have clouded human consciousness and replaced God

with an angel—for whom a luciferic angel then sub-
stitutes itself. This luciferic angel will lead human beings
straight into materialism. This mysterious connection is a
result of those proud and egotistic religious faiths which
have no desire to know of anything higher than an angel.
In their boundless arrogance they say that they speak of
God; in fact they are referring to an angel, and in terms
which are less than thorough. It is this boundless arrogance, often represented as humility, that has had such a
hand in bringing about materialism. If we ponder this, we
can gain insight into a remarkable correlation: by falsely
dressing an angel in God's clothing, the human soul
develops a tendency to materialism. Underlying this is an
unconscious egotism, which expresses itself in a disinclination to elevate oneself to knowledge of the world of
spirit; and which expresses itself also in a desire to
establish a direct connection with one's God only through
one's own present resources. If you consider the implications of what I have said, you will gain insight into
much that occurs nowadays. The only means to combat
this misinterpretation of the nature of the divine, is to
become aware of the spiritual hierarchies. Then we can
realize that modern religious faith does not look beyond
the hierarchy of the angeloi ...

This misrepresentation of the angel, which occurs more
or less consciously, leads—also more or less consciously—to a materialistic view of the world: not in
single individuals, but gradually, throughout the epoch.
These are things which still take place consciously within
the soul. But when we come to the relationship of human
beings with the archangel hierarchy, we find a realm of
which people are very unaware; they may, at times, have
a good deal to say about it, but they know next to nothing.
Rather than addressing the whole hierarchy of archangels, people nowadays often relate particularly to *one*
archangel: this is not a clearly expressed adherence, but

an inclination and feeling connection. In the nineteenth century, this bore certain fruits in one area at least: the rise of national identity, which is unconsciously under-pinned by an overview of the interplay of archangels, and the inclination towards just one archangel in particular. Underlying the concept of national identity is an egotism, albeit a social egotism, similar to the inclination towards one specific angel . . .

Similar distortions arise in relationship to the Epoch Spirits. Again, people often attach themselves to the particular Epoch Spirit which represents for them the spirit of their own specific period. Just think for a moment of our efforts, through the science of the spirit, to counter such period-specific egotism. We try to describe the different epochs which follow on from one another, to characterize them and allow them to affect us; we try to broaden our hearts and souls to encompass the whole of earthly evolution, the whole evolution of the cosmos even, so that, to begin with at least in our thoughts, we can establish a connection with the different Epoch Spirits. But people today have no desire to do this . . . When people rechristen their own angel 'God' and are thus brought under the influence of the luciferic angel, they make an error of belief, of faith, of outlook. This is, to some extent, an individual error. The next step can be the aberration of a whole people or folk—but this also still remains confined to human affairs, and its consequences occur within that realm. But when we develop a distorted relationship with the Epoch Spirit, our errors affect the cosmos. And there is a hidden connection between human errors towards the Epoch Spirit and the begin-nings of a cosmic burden which, in a certain sense, humanity will have to carry . . .

The aberrations which the human being commits in regard to the Epoch Spirit play into cosmic events—and the cosmic events rebound upon us. The consequence of the fact that cosmic events begin to play into human life, is a decadence which extends as far as the physical body. We are affected, in other words, by illnesses, mortality and everything that this involves. (Lecture of 26 November 1916, GA 172.)

Humanity will have to learn to take seriously what the Christ Being can tell it through Rudolf Steiner's science of the spirit. In modern Christian faiths, the only words which remain to describe everything of a supersensible nature are the abstract terms 'God' or 'Spirit'. 'Our dear God' has become a blanket-term which, without further distinction, is made directly responsible for all that happens. It is like a small child who, when asked what he sees through the window, replies: 'The world'. The answer is not wrong, but tells us nothing. We can only make some use of the concept 'world' by making distinctions between all the different things which compose it. If I enjoy a delicious cake and would like to know who made it, so that I can thank them, it would not help me much to be told: 'Humanity baked the cake'.

Why should the world of spirit not be infinitely more diverse than the physical world? In the world today, branches of knowledge are continually multiplying in order to investigate, in ever more detail, the infinite complexity of physical life. But in the world of spirit all we have is 'God' and 'Spirit'. This spiritual illiteracy is the great disease of modern humanity. The deepest longing of people today— so deep, in fact, that they are unconsciously afraid of it—is for a knowledge of the realm of spirit that is no less inclusive and sound than our knowledge of matter.

Belief and grace versus knowledge and freedom

Throughout the centuries three kinds of antithesis have arisen; the science of the spirit can help us to see them not as mutually exclusive opposites, but as complementary polarities. The first concerns grace as opposed to freedom. Human freedom has been widely held to be incompatible with the workings of grace. But such a view is a fundamental misconception of both. Any kind of grace that was opposed to human freedom would have a quite 'graceless' effect upon humanity. The human being is the being of freedom; and our capacity to achieve freedom is the highest grace of all. The merciful workings of the Christ Being and of the spiritual hierarchies always serve to bring about the outer and inner conditions necessary to our freedom. Whoever does not grasp freedom, annuls the workings of grace; for him, grace has been in vain. We must therefore see our capacity to realize freedom as the fulfillment of grace, not as its opposite. Grace without freedom would be utter 'disgrace'.

The same is true of the contrast between belief and knowledge. It is quite misconceived to think of these as mutually exclusive. Rudolf Steiner does not subscribe at all to the view that increasing 'knowledge' must lead to a decline in 'belief'. On the contrary, if we truly understand the power of belief we will see that it is strengthened and supported by deepening knowledge. In the lecture of 2 December 1911 (GA 130), he says:

> People today may consider that belief is part of an outdated legacy from the past; yet the living forces of their souls are nourished by this legacy of faith, which has been passed down in the form of old traditions and customs. People are in absolutely no position to reject belief or not, for it is a power, a sum of forces, which belongs to the life forces of the soul itself. Whether we wish to 'believe' or not has nothing to do with it. The life and health of our soul is dependent on the forces which the word 'belief' represents; if the soul cannot believe anything, it becomes withered, barren and forlorn...

Knowledge is only the foundation of belief. We should be aware of this, so that we can increasingly lift ourselves up to the forces of belief which are active in the human soul.

'Grace versus freedom' and 'belief versus knowledge' led to the third pair of opposites: 'freedom versus love'. Human freedom has always been viewed as detracting from people's social concern for one another. Any increase in individual freedom was thought to threaten communal coherence. For the sake of harmonious interaction, therefore, it was thought that each person should curb their own individual aspirations. This is also a grave misconception.

The basic tenet of Christianity is: 'Love thy neighbour as thyself'—neither more nor less. True freedom, the unfolding and developing of one's individual gifts and capacities, can only be experienced when we realize that our talents have a karmic purpose, to help meet the needs of others. This is a central concept of spiritual science: that every human ego draws towards itself, like a magnet, those particular people whose needs his gifts can satisfy and fulfill.

This 'pre-established' harmony is the earthly reflection of what human souls have communally willed and prepared in the spiritual worlds before birth. There is an inherent, reciprocal relationship between the degree of each person's freedom and the degree of their true concern for others. We can only be free to the extent to which we love our neighbour, and vice versa. Wherever people feel that brotherliness is threatened by freedom, bullying and extortion arise; attention is paid only to the needs one wishes another to fulfill, as though these were, in themselves, an absolute right, unconnected to the reality of specific gifts and talents.

Wherever people feel, on the other hand, that concern for others is opposite to, and should be subordinate to, their freedom, egotism appears. Such people desire to develop what they consider to be their talents and fulfill themselves, enforcing this on others, without realizing that real gifts are only those which fulfill the real needs of other people around them. We human beings are not satisfied by a 'fifty-fifty compromise' between freedom and neighbourly love. We are right to desire one hundred per cent of both. When both are truly genuine, they can only be enhanced or diminished together.

The three last dogmas of the Catholic Church

Nothing could better characterize the descent into materialism of Petrine-Christianity than the three latest dogmas proclaimed in the Catholic Church: the Immaculate Conception of Mary, the Infallibility of the Pope, and the Assumption of Mary with body and soul. Before I discuss these three dogmas, I would like to quote what Rudolf Steiner has to say about the historical task of the Catholic Church:

> The magnificent organizational edifice of the Roman Catholic Church represents the last dried-up trickle of the great stream of civilization of the fourth post-Atlantean epoch. It can be accurately proved, in all details, that the Roman Catholic Church carries on the legacy of a tradition from the civilization of the fourth post-Atlantean epoch which, though it had shrunk to a shadow, was still justified up to the middle of the fifteenth century. Of course it is true that just as later fruits of human evolution appear in earlier, rudimentary forms, so earlier shoots survive into a later season; but it is still generally true that the Roman Catholic Church represents something that was appropriate for Europe and its colonies up to the mid-fifteenth century.
>
> The science of the spirit, as we see it, should grasp hold of what is needed for the culture of the fifth post-Atlantean period . . .

An institution whose soul is imbued with such a spirit as this one was can, if it survives, only do battle on behalf of the past. It would be foolish to demand that the Catholic Church should champion the needs of the future. The same institution which embodied the spirit of the fourth post-Atlantean period cannot possibly also embody that of the fifth. The configuration which the Catholic Church became, and in which it spread throughout the civilized world, exercised far greater, more widespread influence than people realize; the organizational structure of the monarchies, for example, even when they were Protestant, were imbued with Roman Catholicism. This influence, which also took other forms—such as the Roman concepts of law and legislation, and the whole phenomenon of Latinate abstraction—belongs to the fourth post-Atlantean period. It is an influence which organizes people according to abstract concepts, and structures their institutions in particular, hierarchical ways. In contrast, the spirit of the fifth post-Atlantean epoch, whose influence we are now helping to shape through the science of the spirit, does not call for a structure organized upon such fixed and abstract principles; it asks, instead, for an ethical individualism in human social life, such as I have described in my book *The Philosophy of Freedom*. The ethical aspects I have characterized there contrast with the social order required by the Roman Catholic Church, in the same way as the science of the spirit contrasts with Roman Catholic theology. (Lecture of 3 June 1920, GA 198.)

For many centuries the church had ceased proclaiming dogmas. Humanity no doubt had some awareness that it was no longer possible, as in earlier times, to experience a real connection with the world of spirit. It therefore seems all the more tragic that suddenly, in the last century and a half, three new dogmas have been instituted which have plunged the Catholic Church into the ultimate abyss of materialism.

These three dogmas represent a closed system: the first (the Immaculate Conception of Mary) refers to the mystery of birth, the second (the Assumption) to the mystery of death, and the third (the Infallibility of the Pope) to the mystery of the ego—to what is the human being's most important reality between birth and death.

The first dogma does not refer to the immaculate conception of Jesus, but of *Mary*. According to this dogma, the mother of Jesus was virginally conceived and born, in other words without 'sin'. The Gospels only speak of the immaculate conception of *Jesus*. This has caused the modern church insuperable difficulties, the resolution of which is sought in one of two ways: either Joseph, the father, has nothing biologically to do with the whole thing; or else Jesus was conceived and born in the same way as everybody else. The first interpretation is the more 'conservative' one, the second more 'liberal'. The first must conclude that the Gospel text lies—for the line of Jesus' descent clearly passes through Joseph—in order to demonstrate that Jesus is 'of the house of David'. The second view is equally untenable, for the Gospel text clearly states that Mary 'knows not a man' and conceives from the Holy Spirit.

This all begs the question: How did the church come to consider biological fact as sinful? That this came about is obvious from the fact that the biological role of Joseph is excluded, in order to remove any taint of sin. This can only derive from seeing the realm of matter as a place of sin. It was the view of pre-Christian religions that involvement with the material world signifies a muddying of the clear waters of the spirit. Man's redemption was therefore seen in terms of freeing oneself from matter.

But this conviction is also, paradoxically, the very essence of materialism. Materialism ascribes reality and causality only to matter; it sees all human spiritual capacities as an effect of matter. Because the Catholic Church assumes matter to be a more powerful principle than spirit, it is only able to distance the mother of Jesus from 'sin' by concluding that material laws were not at work in her conception.

Rudolf Steiner has a quite different view of the virgin birth. The biological and physical realm belongs to the world of the Father; it is divinely willed and has nothing to do with human morality. The reality of 'original sin' in the moral sense is apparent in egotistic desires and passions which the act of procreation evokes in the consciousness of the parents. The impulse of egotism has arisen to balance out the sacrifice which is required of the parents of an individual who incarnates. If, as in the case of Jesus, ego- tistic desires and passions were excluded, or did not arise, then we have a 'virgin birth'. The act of procreation then takes place in unconscious sleep.

'Virgin' here signifies that no impurity occurs on the part of the ones already incarnated; and that the forces of incarnation are exclusively—that is, in a pure and virginal way—guided by the will of the higher ego that wishes to incarnate and fulfill its task. Rudolf Steiner describes the 'Temple Sleep' of ancient times, which often served to bring about such pure incarnations. The parents procreated dur- ing sleep, uninfluenced by their waking consciousness with its desires and passions, which are by nature egotistic and, in that sense, 'sinful'.

If the virgin birth implied an absence of any biological role on the part of the father, then it would not be enough for Mary to have been conceived 'without sin'; we would have to follow a line of 'sinless conceptions' right back to Adam—which would then cancel out the Fall and 'original sin'. This would, in turn, annul all human evolution—we would be back at the beginning and would have to start all over again.

The second dogma states that Mary was assumed into heaven with body and soul. It is not easy to imagine this—

how does such a body appear, that is transported to heaven? We cannot think of her ascending in the full bodily flesh; but neither can we imagine her transfigured like the Christ Being, for His Resurrection is a unique event. He is a divine Being, whereas Mary is a human being. His Resurrection is testimony to His divine nature. So then we must ask ourselves what view the Church holds about the *Resurrection* itself.

If, at Easter time, we were to listen to a hundred Catholic or Protestant sermons in order to find out about the nature of the Resurrection, we would be able to sum up everything we had heard in a single phrase: Christ is not dead, He lives on. Yet this statement has nothing to do with Christ's Resurrection. For it is true of *all* people: everyone continues to live after their death. In the Gospels, in contrast, the central issue in the Resurrection is that of the *physical body*, of the empty grave.

The dogma of Mary's bodily Assumption is an attempt to 'eternalize' matter, since the moral courage is lacking to affirm its transience. We can only do this when we experience the real, living nature of the spirit, whose evolutionary task is to resurrect the flesh—that is, to *spiritualize* matter.

Because of the conviction that we live only once, this single life is made responsible for 'eternal' damnation or 'salvation'. I know many Catholics who, rightly, find it very hard to come to terms with the idea of 'eternal hell'. In fact, the passage in Matthew (25,46), which is frequently quoted to substantiate this idea—'And these shall go away into everlasting punishment: but the righteous into life eternal.'—should be translated in a totally different way. The *opposite* of 'everlasting' and 'punishment' is to be found in the Greek text: 'Αιώνιος (aionios) means 'for the period of an aeon'—this is not eternity; it refers to a time period, such as that between death and a new birth. κόλασις (Kolasis) means 'maiming', in the sense of unfulfilled potential—that is, the overall consequence of sins of *omission*; everything that one has not achieved, but could have done if one had exercised freedom. This is not a punishment but something we 'inflict' upon ourselves. This is emphasized by the preceding 'judgement', in which Christ draws attention to all the things people have *not* achieved or done: 'For I was an hungred, and ye gave me no meat: I was thirsty, and ye gave me no drink,' etc.

The final judgement at the end of a single life was applied also to positive attainments. After Mary's *single* lifetime she is graced with absolute perfection and fulfillment. This grace is not *worked for* (yes, grace needs to be worked for, as well as being given) through constant work upon herself in many incarnations, in freedom—that is, in a human, individual way. The Mary who is assumed into the heavens is no longer involved in evolution; her development has, one may say, been terminated—or fulfilled if you prefer. If we are to think of her bodily nature as having been spiritualized, this cannot be due to her free endeavour but to a miraculous intervention of God; the laws of human existence are not, in this scenario, gradually transformed through the course of evolution by the free, active involvement of the human being, but suddenly and miraculously anulled and put out of action.

The dogma of the Pope's infallibility is the final seal set upon humanity's struggle over its relationship to the world of spirit. Since the human being has been deemed incapable of forging a direct and individual relationship with the world of spirit, someone must have the 'ex-officio' role of establishing and maintaining this relationship. It is not enough for the church in general to maintain such a connection through its doctrines and rites. It was thought necessary to safeguard the power of the church by assigning this connection with the spiritual world to a single, actual person, thereby making it more precise and binding.

The Pope as 'vicar of Christ' and of the church is declared infallible; in fact he declares *himself* to be so, in the '*ex cathedra*' utterances which he makes. The church asserts that only truths which are already accepted by all Christian faithful are declared to be dogmas. It is untenable to say, though, that such a feeling for the truth of this dogma was present. One is inclined to think that its official sanctioning was more a matter of power than of truth; that it was declared dogma not because it was already accepted but because there was great concern for the fact that it was not.

I have mentioned that this third dogma represents the tragic clouding and darkening of the mystery of the human ego. It is dogmatically decreed that only a single person on the earth—and only because of his office—can establish a real connection with the world of spirit. This means also that no one else can have such a connection. One can hardly imagine a more tragic blasphemy in the whole of human history: a god who created human beings in order to forbid them to have real and direct communication with him.

In Thomas Aquinas' commentary on the St. John Gospel (on the passage in John 4,10 about the conversation with the woman of Samaria), we read that every person—not only the Pope—is called upon to experience and activate the divine spirit within himself:

There are two kinds of water: living and not living. Water that is not living has lost its direct connection with the source from which it originally sprang. It is separated from its fount—the rain, or other source—and kept in pools or cisterns. Living water, on the other hand, is water that retains a direct connection with its origin, continuing to pour forth from it. This is why the grace of the Holy Spirit is also rightly named Living Water: *the grace of the Holy Spirit is given to us in such a way that the source itself of grace—the Holy Spirit—is given . . . This is why, if someone should have the grace of the Holy Spirit but not the*

*Spirit itself, the water would not stream directly from its original source—it would therefore not be living but dead.**

The central thread of Rudolf Steiner's science of the spirit is an awareness that every person is *a being of spirit* in an absolutely real sense. Divine love has done all in its power to *enable* us to experience our own spiritual nature through intuitional thinking. We can therefore understand why Rudolf Steiner, to the end of his life, pointed towards his *Philosophy of Freedom* as the foundation essential for grasping spiritual science.

---

* quia ita ipsa gratia Spiritus sancti datur homini quod tamen ipse fons gratiae datur, scilicet Spiritus sanctus ... Et inde est quod si aliquis donum Spiritus sancti habeat, et non spiritum, aqua non continuatur suo principio, et ideo est mortua, et non viva.

3
THE HISTORY OF 'CHRISTIAN' CHRISTIANITY

So far I have described various aspects of traditional Christianity which inevitably led humanity deeper into materialism. But this is only one part of the history of Christianity over the past two thousand years. Rudolf Steiner's science of the spirit makes clear that something of no less importance was taking place and being prepared during this Petrine-phase. The most important reality to be considered here is connected with the Christ Being Himself, the Risen One, and the way in which He has accompanied humanity over these two thousand years. Christ's super-sensible workings allowed, alongside the 'official' church, an *esoteric* Christianity to arise; this was present as an underground stream within cultural life. Whenever it tried to surface in 'heretical' movements and exert a cultural influence, it was suppressed by officialdom. In addition to the influence of Christ Himself, and esoteric Christianity, there is a third factor at work in this history of 'positive' Christianity: the scholasticism of the Middle Ages, which culminated in the philosophy of Thomas Aquinas. We will see how this phenomenon of exoteric Christianity is also, in its deeper significance, simultaneously esoteric.

The teaching of the Risen One

Among Rudolf Steiner's most beautiful legacies to humanity are his descriptions of the teaching of the Risen Christ, which He gave to his most intimate, initiated pupils. Only after His death was Christ able to tell His disciples of what He had learned and experienced by passing through it. Volume 211 of Steiner's Collected Works (GA) is dedicated to this Mystery. In what follows, Rudolf Steiner tries to find words to express what Christ communicated at that time:

> The human body has gradually become so dense, the forces of death in the human being have become so strong, that he can, it is true, now develop his intellect and exercise freedom. This is only possible in life which passes through the clear transition of death, in which death makes a clear-cut incision, in which, during waking consciousness, awareness of the eternal soul is extinguished. But still you may take up into your souls a certain wisdom: the wisdom which consists in the knowledge that something was fulfilled within my own Being (so spoke the divine teacher, the Christ, to His initiated pupils), something with which you may imbue yourselves if only you can lift yourselves up to see that Christ descended from unearthly spheres to earthly humanity; if only you can lift yourselves up to perceive that there resides upon earth something which cannot be perceived with earthly means, that can only be perceived by means of faculties higher than earthly ones; if you can perceive the Mystery of Golgotha as a divine Event which was planted into earthly life, if you can perceive that a God passed through the Mystery of Golgotha. Of everything else which takes place upon the earth you can derive earthly wisdom. But this would be of no use to you in understanding what death means for human beings— it would only be of use if you could have, like the people of ancient times, no intense interest in death. Since you cannot do otherwise than be interested in death, you must strengthen your understanding with a power stronger than all earthly understanding, one so strong that it can say: the Mystery of Golgotha is something that

broke all natural, earthly rules. If you take up into your faith only the things which abide by natural laws, you will, it is true, be able to see death; but you will never grasp its significance for human life. But if you can raise yourselves up to see that the earth has received, at the mid-point of its evolution, sense and purpose from the Mystery of Golgotha, if you can see that something occurred then which is of a divine nature, that cannot be understood with earthly understanding—then you are preparing in yourselves a special power of wisdom, a power which is the same as that of belief, a particular Sophia-power or power of wisdom and belief. For a strong power of the soul is expressed if one can say: I believe, I know by means of belief, what I could never know and believe with earthly means. This is a stronger power of soul than is possible by confining oneself to knowledge gained through earthly means. Those people are weak whose wisdom consists only in grasping hold of the knowledge that can be gained by earthly means— even if their knowledge encompasses all things on earth. A much greater degree of inner activity must be called upon by anyone who wishes to raise himself to the insight that the supersensible is active within the world of the senses. (The Hague, 13 April 1922, GA 211.)

The Risen One did not only instruct people then; He continues to speak supersensibly everywhere and at all times, for He is the Logos, the cosmic word that continually gives utterance. Where, though, are the people who can hear His spiritual voice? Through His own death Christ gained knowledge of why human beings fear death so much. They become so dependent upon, and immersed in, the physical body that they fear they will experience nothing more once they have cast it off. In the Graeco-Roman period, people had come to identify so deeply with matter that Achilles, speaking to Odysseus, could sum up the state of humanity in the following single phrase, which Rudolf Steiner never tired of mentioning: 'Better a beggar on earth than a king in the realm of shades'. (*Odysee*, canto 11.)

In the bodiless state after death, human consciousness had indeed become dark and shadowy. Human beings had increasingly lost their atavistic clairvoyance, were increasingly incapable of having a real experience of the spirit, had thus become spiritually very 'poor' upon earth. Christ affirms this poverty as necessary to evolution: the prerequisite for each individual being able to *seek* the spirit is grasping freedom and thus becoming a spiritual beggar.

In the first of the Beatitudes (Matthew 5,3), the original Greek uses these very words: 'Blessed are the beggars of spirit' (Μακάριοι οἱ πτωχοὶ τῷ πνεύματι: Makarioi hoi ptochoi to pneumati). The poverty itself is not as important as the *begging* which it requires. To enter the state of beggarhood, three things are necessary: 1. To have nothing; 2. To know this; 3. To wish to overcome this state. This threefold condition encompasses the whole sense and purpose of humanity's evolution: 1. To lose everything which was given by divine grace; 2. To become aware of our spiritual poverty; 3. To become, like Parsifal, questing, individual and freedom-seeking human beings. This trinity: sundering, turning-point, return, is inherent, for example, in the parable of the prodigal son (Luke 15, 11–32) who 'was lost and is found'.

Because each person had become, for the sake of achieving freedom, a beggar of spirit; because in the body-free state after death, no one could any longer be a king in the supersensible realm, preferring to be a beggar on earth—the king of the spirit realm left His sun domain in order to live as a beggar of spirit before the eyes of humanity:

> ... so it became apparent, in the fourth post-Atlantean epoch, that there existed a contemporary form of religion

whose impulse could endow people with the sense that there is an aspect of this physical world which is really an affair of the divine; and which was living proof that what the Greeks had hitherto believed—that it was better to be a beggar in the upper world than a king in the realm of shades—was not so. For now the Greeks came to know the One who had descended from divine realms, and who had fulfilled His destiny amid humanity as a beggar upon earth. This was the answer to the feeling which had reigned during the fourth post-Atlantean epoch. (Lecture of 17 April 1912, GA 143.)

'Spiritual economy'

Through His mighty supersensible teachings the Risen One thus inaugurated His on-going influence within humanity; in the same way, the Christ-bearer, Jesus of Nazareth, left humanity the legacy of the three bodily sheaths which he had offered as a vessel for Christ. There is a spiritual law which Rudolf Steiner calls the law of 'spiritual economy'. If we can become aware of it, this law allows us a deep insight into the real spiritual history of Christianity. This is how Rudolf Steiner sums up spiritual economy:

What we have now spoken of—the fact that the bodily sheaths of a human being who becomes the bearer of a descending Avatar being are multiplied and transposed to others and are reproduced as reflections of the original—is of very particular significance when we come to consider Christ's appearance on the earth. Because the Avatar Christ dwelt in the body of Jesus of Nazareth, it was possible for Jesus' etheric and astral bodies to be multiplied innumerable times; this occurred with the ego also, as an impulse kindled in the astral body of Jesus when Christ entered his threefold bodily sheaths. (Lecture of 15 February 1909, GA 109/111.)

The effect within Christianity of this multiplying of Jesus' *physical body* continued up until the time of Augustine. In these first centuries, therefore, the physical and historical event of Golgotha stands in the foreground. Emphasis is laid upon eye-witnesses of this event. In the second century after Christ, people still based their knowledge upon teachers whose teachers had been taught by the apostles themselves, from whom memories had been preserved even of the Lord's tone of voice and His physical appearance.

Following on from this initial period, up until about the twelfth century, the bearers of Christianity assimilated copies of the *etheric* body of Jesus of Nazareth. This is, according to Rudolf Steiner, the only way to really understand such a phenomenon as the 'Heliand' poem. The poet displays a direct knowledge of the event of Golgotha, as though he had had a kind of Pauline revelation. This becomes comprehensible through the occult knowledge that he bore within himself a copy of Jesus of Nazareth's etheric body.

In the subsequent period, up to the fifteenth century, Jesus' *astral* body was assimilated by the leading adherents of Christianity. We can only understand someone like Francis of Assisi when we realize that he bore within himself the *sentient soul* forces of Jesus of Nazareth. The same is true of Elisabeth von Thüringen. The cultural stream of scholasticism—which will be discussed later—can, when we realize that its chief proponents bore within themselves a reflection of the *mind soul* of Jesus of Nazareth, be understood as an expression of the esoteric workings of the Christ Being. Medieval mysticism later arose in people who bore within themselves reflections of Jesus' *consciousness soul*. Since the sixteenth century it is the *ego* of Jesus which has taken effect. Until now, only the egotistic and materialistic aspect of this ego principle has come to expression. But we now live in a time in which the ego must be formed into an organ receptive to Christ:

Since the sixteenth century we live in a culture of ego-tism. What now needs to be added to this ego-principle? Christian evolution has passed through stages representative of the outer physical body, then of the etheric and astral bodies, and finally of the ego. Now it must assimilate into this ego the Mysteries and secrets of Christianity itself. It must become possible to make the ego into an organ receptive to the Christ, now that it has learnt, through Christianity, to wield the thinking intellect and to apply it to the outer world. This ego must now find its way back to the fount of wisdom of the great Avatar Christ. And how must that come about? Through a deepening of Christianity by means of the science of the spirit ... Christ and Christianity must become the central focus of the emancipated ego of modern times.

We see, then, how Christianity has gradually evolved towards what it must become ... it learnt ego-thinking, learnt to observe the outer world objectively; now it is ready to perceive in all phenomena of this outer world the spiritual realities which are so intimately interwoven with the central Being, the Christ Being. It is ready to perceive Christ underlying all the myriad outer forms of the world.

This is the starting-point for our spiritual-scientific understanding and perception of Christianity; it is the mission and task of our movement, which strives for knowledge of the spirit. We must recognize the reality of this mission. Just as each individual has physical, etheric and astral bodies and ego, and gradually advances to ever loftier heights, so Christianity itself also passes through such an evolutionary process. Christianity also has, one may say, a physical, etheric and astral body and an ego—an ego which can deny its origin in just the same way as does the egotistic ego of our time. Yet it is also an ego which can take up into itself the true being of Christ, and climb upwards to ever loftier heights of existence. (Lecture of 15 February 1909, GA 109/111.)

Esoteric Christianity

Christ Himself is the true essence of Christianity: His unmediated influence within humanity is Christian in the truest sense; and just as there exists a history of the Christ Being's direct influence, so we can also describe the real history of esoteric Christianity. I have already mentioned that esoteric Christianity was initially compelled to go underground, in order to allow Petrine-Christianity to accompany humanity during the period of its deepest descent into materialism. It is the task of the science of the spirit to shed more light upon these little-known underground streams. I can only briefly refer to a few such phenomena.

Paul himself gave Dionysius the Areopagite the task of founding an esoteric school of Christianity in Athens. Not until the sixth century were the orally disseminated teachings of this school written down. This resulted in the writings of the so-called pseudo-Dionysius.

> This Christian esoteric teaching was conducted alongside the outer, exoteric teachings. I have often drawn attention to the fact that Paul, the great apostle of Christianity, made use of his immense and fiery gift for speaking to teach Christianity to the masses; but that he also, simultaneously, founded an esoteric school under the leadership of Dionysius the Areopagite, who is mentioned in the Acts of the Apostles (17,34). In this Christian esoteric school at Athens, founded by Paul himself, the purest form of spiritual science was taught. (Lecture of 19 May 1908, GA 103.)

Other important phenomena of esoteric Christianity were

the schools of initiation into the Irish and Scottish Mysteries. These initiates were able to experience humanity's redemption at the same time as the Event of Golgotha took place. It was they who brought to the Germanic peoples a different form of Christianity from the one that later spread from Rome.

> Over in Asia the Mystery of Golgotha was taking place; in Jerusalem the event was occurring whose historical aspect was later reported in the Gospels in the traditional way. But the initiates of the Hybernian Mysteries knew of the tragic fulfillment of the Mystery of Golgotha in Palestine at the very moment that it occurred, although no word had reached them about it, nor did they know of it through any outer means. Simultaneously with the event itself, the initiates in the Hybernian Mystery centres perceived its reflection in symbolic imagery. In these centres, schooling was not based upon tradition; initiates learnt to perceive the Mystery of Golgotha through the spirit. In Palestine, this majestic, supreme event had taken place in outer, physical reality; in the Mysteries of Hybernia the rites were fulfilled through which the living image of the Mystery of Golgotha could arise there in the astral light. (Lecture of 29 December 1923, GA 233.)

While, in Rome, Christ's words: 'My kingdom is not of this world' were being turned on their head, in the North a spiritual Christianity arose which flowed on in the Grail-stream and, at the end of the Middle Ages, was absorbed into Rosicrucianism.

This is how Rudolf Steiner describes it in his lecture of 31 December 1923 (GA 233):

> ... the physical manifestation of the Mysteries declined more and more. The outer Mystery centres—the places of meeting between God and man—increasingly lost their significance. By the thirteenth and fourteenth centuries

after Christ, there was very nearly nothing left of them. Whoever wished, for example, to seek the Holy Grail, needed to know how to follow spiritual paths. Physical paths belonged to ancient times, before the burning of Ephesus. In the Middle Ages, the paths one followed had to be spiritual ones.

Spiritual paths had especially to be followed—already in the thirteenth and fourteenth centuries, but particularly from the fifteenth century onwards—in the pursuit of a real Rosicrucian training. The Rosicrucian temples were deeply concealed from outer, physical perception. True Rosicrucians visited these temples, which were invisible to normal, outer vision. Pupils, though, who could hear the gods speaking in a gentle look of the eyes, were able to find their way to the old Rosicrucians; here and there such people could be found—hermits imbued with knowledge, with purity of intent and action. I am not speaking in parables—such things were very real and significant in the times to which I am referring. One could find one's way to a Rosicrucian Master only by developing the capacity to hear the language of the heavens in the physical look of another's gentle eyes. Particularly in the fourteenth and fifteenth centuries one could find these remarkable individuals—in the most humble surroundings—whose inner life was pervaded by the divine, who were inwardly connected with the spiritual temples which existed, but which were really as difficult to gain entry to as the Holy Grail of the famous legend.

Rudolf Steiner's science of the spirit follows on from these Rosicrucian streams in a direct, esoteric way; it is, in the deepest sense, a renewal of esoteric Christianity.

The appearance of legends and sagas has an important connection with this inner form of Christianity—which could not, for the time being, exert any influence on general cultural life. Legends can express the deepest evolutionary truths through images, yet without infringing upon people's freedom. Such, for example, is the legend of Barlaam and Josaphat, ascribed to 'John of Damascus'. It tells how the Indian Josaphat—in other words the Bodhisattva as successor of the Buddha—is converted to Christianity by the Christian, Barlaam. This story should be taken seriously, for it describes the real, spiritual confluence of Buddhism with Christianity. Another legend that was widespread and well-loved in Europe during the Middle Ages, is that of the Wandering Jew (Ahasverus), which I will come back to later.

Scholasticism—the Fall and the redemption of thinking

Traditional Christianity shows its most positive justification in the flowering of scholasticism in the Middle Ages. Rudolf Steiner repeatedly emphasized that neither before nor since was the art of thinking carried to such heights, nor sharpened into such a fine instrument. The value of the philosophy of Thomas Aquinas consists at least as much in the method and uncompromisingly honest nature of his thinking as in his conclusions—which are remarkable enough in themselves. These scholars were wholly immersed in the element of thinking.

Rudolf Steiner felt a deep need to describe, in a short series of lectures, the salient aspects of Thomas Aquinas' philosophy. You can find these in volume 74 of the Complete Edition (GA). (I myself belong to the last generation— before the Second Vatican Council took place—to have made a thorough study of Thomas Aquinas. In my day, we still attended lectures in Latin. This was called the neo-Thomistic school. The place where we lived was called the 'Scholasticate', and we ourselves were named 'Scholastics'. After the Council, much changed; Thomas Aquinas ceased being of such central importance.)

These medieval thinkers saw the Fall and 'Original Sin' in a quite different light from the usual moralizing one. They considered the Fall to be far more a matter of consciousness and intellect than of morality. It was clear to them that consciousness is the prerequisite for both good and bad, and that 'Original Sin' had in fact created the conditions necessary for plucking the fruits of the tree of knowledge. What concerned them was the Fall of the intellect—the inability of human thought to penetrate the deepest mysteries of the spiritual, divine world.

As they saw it, human thinking can, by itself, only get to a certain point. What lies beyond its reach has to be communicated to the human being by means of divine revelation, has to be accepted as an act of faith. Human reason can still just about 'prove' the existence of God; but by its own power alone it is incapable of perceiving that God consists of a trinity, that the Son aspect of this trinity incarnated in order to redeem humanity, that through the transubstantiation bread becomes the body of Christ.

The 'intellectual Fall' consists, for these thinkers, in the fact that the human intellect has 'sundered' itself from direct and real experience of the spirit. The question of redemption was thus also seen in terms of consciousness, not morality: for if human thinking is unable to alter the fact that it is sundered from the spirit, this cannot be considered morally sinful. Human longing for redemption became for these scholastics a longing for the redemption of *thinking*. If we can be redeemed at all, they believed, it must first be through our thinking.

The scholastics, though, could not have expressed these thoughts in such terms, which derive from the science of the spirit. But they experienced them, nonetheless, as questions in the depths of their souls. Rudolf Steiner expressly points us towards these half-conscious, but inwardly suffered, questionings of the scholastics. Thomas and Albertus, for example, both sensed the tragedy inherent in the extreme position of some thinkers, who asserted that the human intellect had fallen so far that it could arrive at 'truths' which stood in direct opposition to revealed truth, and as such were in fact wholly fallacious. Thomas and Albertus opposed this view. Their trust in human thinking, their tireless championing of reason, led them to such a high opinion of the power of the human spirit that they felt this assertion to be untenable, even blasphemous. This touches on the controversy of 'double truth', of which Rudolf Steiner says:

> This question glimmers in the under-depths of the soul; in the souls of Albertus and Thomas also: Do we not also bear original sin within our thinking, within our faculties of reason? Is it not because reason has fallen away from spirituality that it deceives us with illusory, not real truth? Only if we take Christ into our reason, thereby transforming it and allowing it to evolve further, does this reason enter into harmony with the truth which is inherent in faith and belief.
>
> The idea of reason's sinfulness underpinned, to some degree, the concept of 'two truths' in the period preceding Albertus and Thomas. Thinkers earnestly desired to combine the teachings about original sin with those of redemption. They did not yet possess the logical power of thought to enable them to do this, but that was what they sought to do. They posed this question: How does Christ redeem our power of reason, which contradicts spiritually revealed truth? How can we become Christian through and through? (Lecture of 23 May 1920, GA 74.)

This search for the redemption of human thinking was at the same time a striving to find the immortal kernel of human individuality. The Arabian Aristotelians, especially Averroës, had asserted that there is only a universal mind. A drop of this cosmic reason separates from the universe and combines with the body at birth. At death it is reabsorbed into the unity—there can, therefore, be no question of individual immortality. The scholastics interpreted Aristotle in a quite different way: the Christian perspective brought about a need to see the human being as a spiritual *individual* and ego; without this, the idea of moral responsibility for one's own actions cannot be sustained.

This is one example of the decisive influence which the Christ Impulse had within humanity. If we are to be spiritual individuals after death, we must also be so during life. Our spirit's connection with the body allows individuality to arise through awareness of ourselves as separate egos. As it connects with the body's mirror of itself, the ego becomes conscious—it has an authentic experience of itself as ego, which can then also persist in a world of pure spirit, without the body. An ego-being that is not yet conscious of itself has not yet entered into full egohood and individuality (cf. the beginning of chapter 9 of Rudolf Steiner's *The Philosophy of Freedom*).

The scholastics did not yet have the perspective necessary for solving the question of the redemption of thinking and individual immortality; human consciousness had not yet become capable of applying an overall view to such questions. The idea of *evolution*, which has already been mentioned, was not present in a fully-fledged form; the fact alone that knowledge of repeated incarnations had been lost was enough to encourage a more static—as opposed to a dynamic—view of the human being. These thinkers, therefore, held fast to ideas about the intellect and immortality which were more concerned with fixed conditions than with a dynamic, evolutionary approach.

Not until the science of the spirit of our own time arose did it become possible to realize that the millennia of evolution are working towards *attaining*, in freedom, the redemption of thinking, and towards *gaining* individual immortality. The answer of the science of the spirit to the

question of the redemption of thinking which the scholastics wrestled with, and carried with them over the threshold
of death, is both simple and staggering: human thinking is
redeemable, in other words, it can *evolve.* Because the goal of
evolution and of the human being is to attain freedom, and
because freedom is inherent in thinking itself, human
beings cannot expect to be redeemed or set free by means of
grace alone. The only true redemption for human beings
lies in their *potential* for freedom, not in a gift from above.
Our freedom is inherent in the task of realizing this
potential.

Thinking is not so much there to reflect outer reality as to
enable us to develop towards our true, free humanity. Just
as the essence of the wheat kernel does not lie in its nutritional value, but in the life forces from which a new plant
springs up, the nature of thinking does not lie in its connection with outer reality but in what we human beings can
become by means of it.

And just as the fact that we eat the plant should have
absolutely no influence on our description of its nature
and growth, so the knowledge we can gain by means of
the evolutionary impulse at work within us should not
become the basis of a theory of knowledge; we must be
clear that what we ordinarily call knowledge is a side-
effect of the workings of thinking within our human
nature. Then we can approach the true essence of this
thinking. It is at work within us. The false teachings of
nominalism, and of Kant, only arose because the question
of knowledge was approached in the same way as one
would approach a study of the nature of wheat from the
point of view of nutritional science.

We can say, therefore, that when we recognize what
Thomism can mean in our own time, and how it shoots
up again from what formed its most central kernel in
medieval times, then we will find it sprouting again in the

science of the spirit of the twentieth century. (Lecture of 24 May 1920, GA 74.)

Through the fact that individuality *arises* essentially through the exercising of freedom and creativity in thinking, the spiritual nature of the individual human being is at the same time invoked in the ethical sphere. As thinking itself becomes a moral deed of freedom and of the highest moral responsibility, the individual experiences the power of thinking, upon which his actions are based, as moral imagination and intuition. There arises what Rudolf Steiner calls *ethical individualism* in the second part of *The Philosophy of Freedom*: we do not act as free individuals as a matter of course, but we can *become* free in our actions.

The full depth and significance of the Mystery of the transubstantiation, which was mentioned earlier, can only really be understood in this context. The redemption of thinking is at the same time thinking's permeation with Christ. Christ makes possible the consecration, the transubstantiation within thinking. Every single person has the capacity to experience the spirit, through thinking, as more substantial than what can be perceived through the senses. Substantial here means truly active, of real effect. We are unfree when we experience the causal effect of matter; then it becomes so substantial to us that it exerts a near-total influence on our spirit—we become *its* effect. Through the transubstantiation of our own being which can be achieved by living, active thinking's evolutionary power, *thinking* itself acquires the most real substantiality and essence, gracing also all other things with reality and substantiality. In dead, passive thought, the human being lives in a pre-Christ condition—of pre-transubstantiation and pre-freedom. In living thinking, both the human being and the world are transubstantiated. Wherever we gain access to the spirit in thinking, all things acquire their spiritual substantiality.

4
THE FUTURE OF CHRISTIANITY
THROUGH THE SCIENCE OF THE SPIRIT

All our observations up to this point have been concerned with the two aspects of Christianity that developed over the last two thousand years. I would now like to look forwards and ask: Does Christianity have a future—and if so, what is it? What is the future task of Rudolf Steiner's science of the spirit in respect to Christianity?

Rudolf Steiner's central thought about the Christ Being and Christianity can, as I have already mentioned, be formulated as: *Christianity and humanity are one and the same thing.*

The Christ Being did not embody a super-human or extra-human, let alone an unhuman principle; He was the fulfilment and embodiment of the evolutionary potential present in every person. Christ Himself never used the word 'Christian'; he had no need to. He named Himself 'Son of Man', really so as to draw the distinction with 'Son of God'. In the language of those days, 'Son of God' meant everything that had been divinely created and formed by God the Father. As 'Son of God', the human being is not yet independent or self-reliant; he is only a receiver of grace, an effect of divine workings.

It is not until the 'Son of Man' arises—everything created and formed in freedom by the human being himself—that the free human being comes into his own. The purpose of evolution is for the Son of God to be transformed eventually into the Son of Man. Every being is, at the outset of its evolution, a 'creature'; only gradually does it evolve into a co-creator. At the mid-point of evolution, humanity had sunk to such depths that it killed the 'Son of Man' and gave life to 'Barabbas'. In Aramaic, 'Barabbas' means 'Son of the Father'. This term refers to someone who makes no contribution of his own, just carries on what his father passed down to him. Pupils in the Mysteries were called 'Barabbas'—in other words they were 'sons of the father' in the sense of 'sons of the teacher'. The pupil was so true to his guru-teacher that he just reflected his spirit.

Christianity's historical form, which has until now been so influential in western culture, was not nearly Christian enough in the pure, human sense. When Rudolf Steiner speaks of a return to esoteric Christianity, he means that Christianity will only have a future by embodying ever more fully all that is universal and human.

> ... we need today to return to a knowledge of esoteric Christianity. We need to know that there is more to Christianity than its exoteric aspect, although the Gospels can give us an inkling of unseen depths. People do not speak much about esoteric things nowadays. But humanity must find its way back to a source which can hardly be traced in outer records; anthroposophical spiritual science must help us see further, into the teachings which Christ Himself gave to His initiated pupils after His Resurrection. These could only be given after He had passed through an experience on earth which He could not have passed through in higher, divine worlds, for until the Mystery of Golgotha death did not affect divine beings ... (Lecture of 2 April 1922, GA 211.)

The resurrection impulse contained in Rudolf Steiner's *The Philosophy of Freedom*, which describes how the human being can, in thinking, have his own inner experience of the drama of death and resurrection, is central to esoteric Christianity. In the same lecture, Rudolf Steiner continues:

> We must try to develop a sense for the fact that, in

thinking, we are not really alive—that we are pouring our life into the mould of dead, logical pictures; and that we need to develop strong life-forces to resurrect this dead reasoning. Then we can begin to feel the creative life within it, and gain access to the realm from which moral impulses arise through the power of pure thought—through which we can also learn to understand the nature of human freedom.

I tried to describe this in my *Philosophy of Freedom*. This book points to a morality which arises when dead thoughts are revitalized, resurrected, to become moral impulses. Such a freedom-philosophy is therefore wholly in accord with inner Christianity.

I wanted, today, to put these considerations of esoteric Christianity before you. In our time, in which there is so much dispute about exoteric and historical Christianity, it is necessary to point to these esoteric Christian teachings. (Lecture of 2 April 1922, GA 211.)

For a renewal of *esoteric* Christianity, an awareness is necessary of the ongoing *continuity* of the Mystery of Golgotha, in a threefold sense: cosmic, mystic and historical. The cosmic dimension is connected with the overall evolution of the earth itself, which is in the process of being transformed from a planet into a sun, by Christ. The earth's destiny is wholly interwoven with this cosmic Christianity. The mystic dimension is connected with the evolutionary stages of human inner life and consciousness. The inner evolution of humanity is, at the same time, the evolution of the spiritual inwardness of the earth, and of the Christ Being Himself. The historical dimension is connected with the dynamic of reciprocal influence between the cosmic and mystic dimensions. This dynamic produces the actual reality of evolution; what we call history is an aspect of this total evolution.

The First and Second Coming

The new phase of Christianity which began with Rudolf Steiner's science of the spirit is inseparable from the Mystery of the Second Coming, which was spoken of already in the New Testament. The difference between the First and Second Coming, and also their connection with one another, is one of the most important aspects of both spiritual science and Christianity. The very fact that the science of the spirit was given to humanity at the beginning of this century is integral to the whole event of Christ's reappearance.

The First Coming was Christ's Deed; the Second Coming is the human being's reply. The Mystery of Golgotha was the deed of His love, which he fulfilled for the sake of all people, independently of any response they might give. At that time He created the conditions in human beings on the basis of which they would be able, later, to respond consciously.

The Second Coming, on the other hand, does not occur at the same time for all people. It is a matter of individual evolution and freedom. In the First Coming, Christ came towards us—descended to us, to the earth. In the Second Coming, human beings need to elevate themselves and go towards Him, to experience His presence in a world of pure spirit. The power of living thinking is also decisive for our experience of the Second Coming; for only through thinking can we—initially at least—experience the reality of spirit.

The Greek word which is usually translated as 'Second Coming' or 'Reappearance' actually has nothing to do with reappearance. The word *parousia* in fact literally means 'being present' (para-eimi) or 'spiritual presence'. The translation, 'Second Coming' or 'Return', encourages the false idea that Christ deserted the earth and humanity, and would later 'come back'. This is not the case: 'I am with you until the end of all cycles of earthly time' means that the

Risen One is always spiritually present. The departure occurs only in human consciousness; human beings distance themselves from Christ, not the other way round. The Second Coming is not a reappearance on His part, but His refinding by human consciousness.

Christ, Lord of Karma

Through this distinction between the nature of the First and Second Coming of Christ, we can understand something else which plays an important role in Rudolf Steiner's science of the spirit: that in our time Christ takes on His function as Lord of karma.

Christ, lord of karma: what does this mean?

Rudolf Steiner tells us that up until our times, Moses helped the human being after death to draw up the balance-sheet of his life. Evolution stood under the sign of divine justice. The law of Moses, the tablets engraved with the Ten Commandments, were the symbol of this. But from the beginning of our century, each person who dies encounters not Moses but Christ. Christ helps each one weigh up his life and prepare his karma or destiny for the next earthly life. This important change means that divine justice provides the basis and conditions for freedom, and that balanced karma will, in future, not be sufficient by itself. The karma of justice is changing into a karma of love. Human beings no longer only ask what they need to do in order to compensate for their own deficiencies; they are also becoming capable of desiring and seeking a balance which will serve all humanity. The fact that Christ has become the Lord of karma does not mean that a unified human karma has only just arisen. This has always existed. Humanity has always been a whole spiritual entity. What is new in our time is the *consciousness* that all people are interwoven with one another. To the extent to which we can experience ourselves, through conscious thinking, as part of all humanity, we can work in freedom towards the mutual reintegration of all human beings in the spirit; this is the task of the second half of evolution. In the lecture of 14 October 1911, from the cycle *From Jesus to Christ* (GA 131), Rudolf Steiner says:

> After passing through the gates of death, we are reincarnated in a later period. So that our karma can be balanced out, certain things must take place; everyone harvests what they have sown. Karma remains a just law. But the fulfilment of karmic law is not confined to each separate individual, it does not compensate for each isolated set of egotisms. Instead, the compensation required by each individual should occur in a way that best serves the totality of humanity's needs. We must balance our karma in a way that most advances the progress of all human beings on the earth. For this we need illumination, not merely the general knowledge that our deeds have karmic consequences which compensate for them. Since some consequences are more helpful than others for all mankind, thoughts and feelings must be chosen which not only resolve our own karma but which are also useful to the whole progress of humanity. It will in future be the task of Christ to integrate our personal balancing of karma with the overall progress of humanity, with the general karma of the earth.

Rudolf Steiner repeatedly describes the decisive influence of the Christ Event in terms of a transition from blood-relationship to relationship based on free choice. Before the time of Christ, blood-forces determined and supported people's thoughts and actions; since Christ, freedom must play an increasing part in the connections we have with each other. In this context, though, freedom means *consciousness*. The Christianity of the Second Coming is one of knowledge and understanding.

Relationship based on free choice depends upon freely developing awareness of who belongs karmically with oneself; and on recognizing the evolutionary potential contained within these karmic connections. At Christ's death on the cross, as the blood flowed from His wounds, the evolutionary law of elective affinity was inaugurated. Christ said to His mother: 'Woman, behold thy son!' And to His disciple: 'Behold thy mother'—although they had no blood-tie with one another. Elective affinity is a relationship of common ideals, the communion of shared idealism. The greater the compass and 'humanity' of a person's ideals, the more his elective affinity will serve mankind.

This perspective of a unity of karma, and of the Being of love as Lord of karma, was lacking in pre-Christian religions. Redemption was seen more as a personal, individual affair. It was not yet possible to regard humanity as a single organism, in which the good of an individual member cannot be separated from the good of the whole. Individuality was still a tender shoot that could not yet recognize and take responsibility for the whole organism of humanity.

It was similar with our relationship to nature and the earth. The human being of pre-Christian religions desired to shake off matter, to detach himself from the earth, without consciously concerning himself with the further destiny of the earth itself and the realms of nature. According to Rudolf Steiner—and this made a very powerful impression on me when I read it—all pre-Christian religions were religions of 'release and redemption', in contrast to Christianity which is, rather, a 'resurrection religion'. This means that in true Christianity there is inherent a sense of human responsibility for the evolution of the earth and nature. It is redemption when human beings are released from the shackles of earth. But it is resurrection when, in the course of evolution, they redeem the whole earth as well as themselves through a process of transformation and spiritualization of the whole of nature itself.

In the following passage, Rudolf Steiner is referring in particular to Buddhism; but what he has to say applies to all pre-Christian religions:

> 'Release from the suffering of existence!' This is of utmost importance in Buddhism. One can truly call it a 'redemption religion', a religion to help people find release from the suffering of existence; and since suffering is inherent in all existence, release from existence as well—in other words, from the repeating cycle of human reincarnation! ...
>
> It would not be right, though—and this is easily shown—to call Christianity a redemption religion in the same sense. A true comparison of Christianity with Buddhism would reveal the former to be a religion of 'rebirth'; Christianity starts from the knowledge that everything in an individual human life bears fruit of significance and value for that person's inmost being, and is carried over with him into a new life, where it is brought to a greater stage of perfection ...
>
> Goethe wished to depict an individual who was aware that everything achieved in earthly life remains and must be woven into the fabric of eternity: 'The traces my earthly days have left, cannot fade for aeons of time!'
>
> That is the true, absolutely real Christian impulse, which leads to the reawakening of spiritualized earthly deeds. That is resurrection religion! (Lecture of 2 December 1909, GA 58.)

Ethical individualism—individualizing the will

The evolution of Christianity has not come to an end—it is only just beginning. What is new about Rudolf Steiner's science of the spirit is not that it automatically makes us 'more Christian', but that it helps us to become aware that we are still at the very beginning both of becoming human and of being permeated by Christ.

When we ask ourselves what it means to be wholly human, we find a dual answer—not only in Steiner, but in the best of traditional Christianity. Being human involves two basic aspects: the *universal* and the *individual*. Every person is human like every other; but is also human in a quite different way to every other. The universal perspective becomes real in our consciousness to the extent to which all humanity is seen and experienced as a unified organism, in an increasingly deep and concrete way. The aspect of individuality is no less a matter of consciousness; it requires of each person an increasingly real identification of ego-consciousness with the true ego being.

The higher ego of every person is an individual member of the spiritual organism of all humanity; each human ego expresses humanity in a singular and unrepeatable way. The power of moral imagination, discussed in the second part of *The Philosophy of Freedom*, encompasses the totality of gifts and talents resonating from each person's eternal being. Every individual can only will to be what his innate forces make him; no one is the same as someone else— otherwise individuality would have no meaning. In Chapter 9 of *The Philosophy of Freedom*, Rudolf Steiner writes:

> *To live* in love of action, and to *let live* in understanding of the other person's (alien) volition, is the fundamental maxim of *free human beings*. They know no other *'ought'* than one with which their volition is in intuitive agreement; how they should act in a particular case their power of ideation will tell them. (GA 4.)*

The will of another person is here described as wholly different or 'alien'. This word is not lightly used. It was

---

* Stebbing revised translation, 1992.

actually added to the 1918 edition of the book. In the addendum to Chapter 10, Rudolf Steiner sums up all that has been said in previous chapters about the polarity between the individual and the universal:

For those who recognize how ideas are intuitively *experienced* as self-existing entities, it is evident that when the human being *cognizes* he enters into the compass of the world of ideas as into something which is the same for all, but when he derives from this idea-world the intuitions for his acts of will, he individualizes a link of that world through *the same activity* which he uses, as a universal one, in the conceptual process of cognition. What appears to be a logical contradiction: the general nature of cognitive ideas and the individual nature of moral ideas, becomes, in fact, when seen in its *reality*, a living concept. It is characteristic of human nature that what is intuitively grasped swings to and fro within the human being like a living pendulum, between universally valid knowledge and the individual experience of this universal element. For those who fail to see one side of the swing, thinking remains only a subjective human activity; for those who fail to grasp the other, all individual life seems lost in the human being's activity of thinking. To the first kind of thinker it is the act of cognition that is unintelligible; to the second kind it is moral life. Both will put forward a variety of notions in order to explain the one or the other, all of which prove inadequate, either because they fail to realize that thinking can be experienced, or they misunderstand it as an activity that merely abstracts. (GA 4.)*

True humanity will arise within mankind to the extent to which each human being comes to individualize himself, realizing his individuality in an increasingly pure and

---

* Stebbing revised translation, 1992.

consistent way. No two individuals can share an identical will. Every individual person is a species of its own. Many people assert that love is an expression of two or more individuals 'wanting the same' as each other. In terms of *The Philosophy of Freedom*, though, this 'identical will' is the essence of immorality. Wherever people 'want the same', individuality is extinguished. Since human individuality consists of the sum both of each person's moral good and of their moral responsibility, we can say with full justification that any prevention or suppression of our potential for individualized will represents the very essence of immorality.

The future of human social order can never consist in people wanting the same as each other. This apparently common will is always the will of one or several that is forced upon the others. Of course people have to accommodate each other, agree upon things so that they can work together. But such agreements are only an outer framework, not an expression of each individual's actual will. Within this larger framework, each person must know his own individual will. If the individual will of each does not come to expression within the outer framework, it remains an empty vessel with no purpose. The enormous difficulties which people experience nowadays in their common work, in their relationships, do not derive from not wanting the same as each other, but from the fact that most of them do not know what they individually want.

Most people look to the common context of the institutions and organizations within which they operate for their individual fulfilment. This is, of course, an absolute contradiction—the group soul cannot possibly fulfil the individual. Those who expect most guidance from a particular institution will be the ones who complain about it and criticize it most. They will always feel disappointed, for it will not be able to provide them with the self-realization that they seek.

Let us imagine a social group of ten people who are involved in a common task—running a school or hospital for example—and that these people are more or less like Goethe and Schiller. How would they run the common project? They would clearly differentiate between two levels of operation. The first is the level of outer framework, which must be formed in common agreement. This belongs very much to the 'corporate will' which we will come back to in a moment. Such a framework will tend to be confined to a minimum, since none of those involved will be looking to it for individual fulfilment. It will serve its purpose if it does not directly hinder each person from developing his individual contribution, but actually makes this possible. Although this outer framework will be minimal—and always open to revision, since it is only a means to an end— it is nevertheless highly regarded and valued, for everyone is aware that it constitutes the *necessary* conditions for each separate person to unfold his individuality. Contravening or ignoring the common agreements will be considered the gravest moral offence. Each person respects the outer framework in a way that is inseparable from respect for each separate individual.

The other level is that of the individual sphere of will-activity of each person. The more a person recognizes and acts upon his true individual will—the will of his higher ego—the more his intentions and actions will differ from those of others. There arises the most wonderful multiplicity and variety of ego-expressions; and it would be quite unthinkable that two individuals should want to will the same, for then they would stop being individuals. What is right and proper for one person at a particular moment is not right and proper for someone else.

For the English-speaking reader I would like to refer to R.W. Emerson by quoting some sentences from his work *Spiritual Laws*. I trust that these sentences will speak for themselves:

... But that which I call right or goodness is the choice of my constitution; and that which I call heaven, and inwardly aspire after, is the state or circumstance desirable to my constitution; and the action which I in all my years tend to do, is the work for my faculties. We must hold a man amenable to reason for the choice of his daily craft or profession. It is not an excuse any longer for his deeds that they are the custom of his trade. What business has he with an evil trade? Has he not a *calling* in his character?

Each man has his own vocation. The talent is the call ... This talent and this call depend on his organization, or the mode in which the general soul incarnates itself in him. He inclines to do something which is easy to him and good when it is done, but which no other man can do. He has no rival, for the more truly he consults his own powers, the more difference will his work exhibit from the work of any other ... Every man has this call of the power to do somewhat unique, and no man has any other call ...

Goethe never expected the court at Weimar to fulfill his individual aspirations. He certainly never thought that everyone else ought to unite with his will, or that he should unite with the will of others. If that had been the case, everyone else would also have had to 'will' a *Faust* or *Wilhelm Meister* into being—and in exactly the same way as Goethe himself. But what is meant by the individualization of the will is precisely this: that a person such as Goethe knows what he wills, out of the overflowing gifts of his individuality. It is clear to him not only that no one else ought to will what he wills, but still more, that no one else *can* do so. The will of the true, higher ego is individual; in other words, it expresses itself in a particular, specific way in each different life-situation. It is the normal, lower ego-consciousness which has difficulty overcoming abstract generalizations and making the individual, moral intuitions of the higher ego its own.

Let us imagine that two teachers have one and the same class with the same pupils. Does this mean that they should have exactly the same aspirations and will—both for themselves and for the pupils—as each other? By no means! Saying that both wish to be teachers, that both of them want the best for their pupils, that both strive to love the children, does not express anything precise and specific. Such statements remain quite abstract and general and can never, by themselves, form the real content of individualized willing.

If we look deeper into the specific, individual sphere of karma, the impulses which dwell in the true ego and will of the one teacher—the inner intentions he has towards each one of his pupils—are quite different from those of the other teacher. Each will teach in quite different ways from the other. If we should examine the different karmic effect upon each pupil of the one or other teacher, and upon each teacher in relationship to every separate pupil, we would find a quite different infinity of influences coming into play, due to the differences between the teachers. 'Consider not only "what", but still more "how" . . .' (*Faust*). The 'what' is the common fact of being teachers; but much more important is the 'how'—the very individual way, as different as two separate worlds—that they each approach their tasks. Only by becoming conscious of this individual 'how' can each person experience his own individuality and fully realize his potential.

Or let us take two people who are man and wife. If they strive to will the same as one another, they remain in a sphere of abstraction; or they control one another—by no means a rare occurrence. In the concrete, individual reality of the realm of will-forces, one of the partners may have formed the intention, before birth, of developing great courage (having, in the previous life, been the soul of gentleness). The other, for individual and opposite reasons, may have undertaken to develop gentleness. Both are wholly and equally justified; and in fact, as man and wife, they may be particularly suited to help each other. Can we say, though, that they have, or should have, one and the same will? Certainly not.

One might object that all those who are striving to develop courage share a common will. But the reply to this must be that there are as many individual forms of courage as there are courageous people. The same is true for every single characteristic, temperament, even for every feeling. One person's joy is never the same as someone else's. The way one person loves is quite different from the way another does. Every person has his own and different form of love, joy, sadness and so forth.

A person can only try to be like another through ego-less imitation. But he then ceases to be what *he* is, and also fails altogether to become what the other is. There are people, for example, who try to imitate St. Francis of Assisi; but the fundamental characteristic of this wonderful man was his total originality—he never imitated others! Only by giving up the wish to be like him, and learning to become wholly original and unique, could one ever begin to resemble him.

At this point one must reply to the objections of a misconceived morality, which asks how people can possibly work together if every individual wills, or ought to will, something different from every other. But just as the future of the free ego depends upon a continually increasing individualization of the will, so the future of society depends upon thinking becoming increasingly universal. Each separate person is completely individual in the realm of moral intuition; but in the sphere of knowledge and thinking we must strive towards unity and agreement. The objectivity of truth is not subject to individual colouring. When we are dealing with the world as it is, rather than the world we intend to create through our will, we can achieve perfect accord through the objectivity of thinking.

At present, humanity encounters great difficulties because most people consider such a communion of truth and objectivity to be too far-fetched and insubstantial an aim. Wherever thinking does not manage to unite people, they strive instead for a commonality of feeling and will impulses. But this 'common ground' is a communion not of the spirit but of nature. The only possible way to achieve true communion with one another is to strengthen the thinking so that it becomes an organ of objective understanding of the phenomena of the world.

Let us imagine for a moment that a community of people had succeeded in purifying their thinking, so that they were united in the objectivity of everything they observed and grasped. These people would experience the deepest joys of common understanding. For a true sense of community is only to be found in objectivity, which is the same for all.

Let us assume that a group of people all come to a shared understanding that something they had intended to do is in fact not attainable, for real and objective reasons. If these people could cease desiring what ran counter to the demands of reality, if they could all affirm its impossibility, out of an inner, thinking acceptance of reality, they would experience both community with one another as well as a high degree of inner freedom.

Rudolf Steiner is often accused of giving too little space to love within his definition of freedom. In *The Philosophy of Freedom*, he speaks of a 'love for one's own deeds'—when we do not act out of physical necessity or emotional urge, but out of an intention that arises through our freedom of spirit. When we act in this way, our deed is one of *pure love*. But in a social, communal context also, freedom can be seen as something that is only perfected through love.

Egotistic freedom is arbitrary. It is negative freedom— freedom 'from'. Positive freedom begins when we are free 'for' something. Inherent in the concept of an organism— and humanity is, in its spiritual reality, a single organism—

is that the individual gifts and characteristics of each
member correspond to the real needs of every other member. If freedom consists in unfolding one's own gifts without hindrance or compromise, the free person is also one
who most loves, for he best serves the needs of others.

The best way of serving others is to do what one does
best, and to leave to others what one cannot do. People who
value love above all else, but who do not rate freedom
highly, can only wish to 'love' others. But this is as empty
and unspecific—in other words abstract—as the search for
'happiness'.

Whoever wants happiness, wants nothing at all; or at
least has not the slightest inkling what his true ego specifically wills. He will never be happy, for happiness comes
as a result of strong, specific intentions which are acted
upon. It is this that Rudolf Steiner wishes to make clear in
the whole thirteenth chapter of *The Philosophy of Freedom*.

It is the same with love. It comes as a result of real freedom, of unfolding the immanence of individuality. Whoever is most *himself*, best serves others. Whoever wishes
only to love, is in love with his love. He takes egotistical
pleasure in his lovingness. Pleasure he may have perhaps,
but not joy. For other people do not want his love to be more
important to him than they are. They want *him*, in his
deepest and truest aspect, for that is what serves them best.

The cosmopolitanism of humanity — the spiritual body of Christ

Rudolf Steiner speaks in his lectures on *The Social Future*
(GA 332a, on October 29 1919) of three basic social forms,
which correspond to the three basic stages of human evolution. In ancient times there existed a social structure
controlled by 'power': a single will—not human but
divine—ruled the social organism. In the age of the

pharaohs, for instance, initiation allowed access to the divine will, and the king imparted this will to the masses. The individual will had not yet awoken within separate human beings.

Rudolf Steiner calls the second stage, in which we still find ourselves today, the 'bargaining society'. In this phase, the individual will has woken within each person: each one carries, as it were, a separate atom of will within himself. But the capacity to harmonize these will-atoms, to integrate them with each other, is hardly developed at all. All the distinct will-directions, therefore, batter against each other; one can only stand back and wait to see what the chance outcome of all these conflicting directions will be.

The third social phase offers the promise of great hope for humanity. Rudolf Steiner calls it the 'communing society'*. He coins a term which does not yet exist; for this stage has, as yet, hardly begun to become reality. In the communing society, the multiplicity of individual will impulses are harmonized with one another, without them being compromised or constrained; the distinctness of every single individual is, as far as possible, supported and encouraged. In the bargaining society by contrast, each person's will is constantly conflicting with and hindering the will of every other person.

In Rudolf Steiner's vision, the communing society is underpinned by a striving to form the 'comprehensive will'—another quite new term: notice that he does not speak of a 'common will', which would mean a return to a single, shared will—as existed in the 'power society'. This primal stage is a state that the church has always desired to return to: for only by striving backwards towards outmoded, theocratic power-structures can the church, as such, retain its coherence. The concept 'comprehensive' or 'total

---

* In German, *Gemeingesellschaft*, which is composed of two terms: *Gemeinschaft*—community, and *Gesellschaft*—society. (Transl.)

will' means something quite different—an integration of the two dimensions: the individual and the social.

To form the total will it is necessary to affirm the individual will of each person, to create a shared, outer framework which allows all individual wills to mutually foster and advance each other. Of course this is a much harder undertaking than reducing everything to a single will. But easier is not better. Freedom is harder than unfreedom, but not worse.

Whenever a 'common task' is spoken of, which an individual is meant to 'serve', there is always a danger that the person in a position of power—whether an official or a dictator—will be tempted to impose his will and aims upon others. However elevated these aims may be, the others are still used as a means to an end.

Another variation of the 'common task', widely used to suppress individuality, are those 'unavoidable forces of circumstance' we are no doubt all familiar with. Great sins have been committed against humanity in the name of such 'forces of circumstance'! As if they could ever provide a moral justification for making human beings into a means to an end.

The two cultural phenomena described by Rudolf Steiner as 'power' and 'bargaining' societies represent the two one-sided extremes of our past evolution. The first was a one-sided unity, but without individual autonomy. The other extreme was a chaotic awakening of individual will, which was very largely responsible for the breaking down of unity and community. This also shows us that two opposing, anachronistic tendencies can hinder the advance of evolution. The first anachronism reverts to the power society, suppressing the individual apparently for the sake of the common good. The second values individual egotism above all and everyone else, and leaves us stuck in the bargaining society.

Individual will means the will of the true ego of every

human being. This will alone is truly individual—as distinct as the eternal core of each person's individuality. But every person also bears within himself the 'will' of the lower ego, the egotistic will. This will should really be called 'wish' or 'desire', for it is ruled by drives and instinct, and as such it is never wholly free: it is 'group-will'— general, abstract and non-specific. Most people usually know what they wish, but seldom what they will. The individualization of the will, as a process of increasing consciousness, has nothing to do with the egotism of the lower ego—for this is actually not individual at all. We can recognize real individuality by its spiritual and intuiting character; which can, in turn, only be grasped by thinking.

I have known many people who saw in the Gospels only an emphasis on love, community and self-sacrifice. Such people ask: Where, in the Gospels, is there any mention of free individuality? But it is only in our own time that consciousness has begun to advance to a stage where free egohood can be appreciated and valued—for only now is it really becoming possible. This means, in turn, that a quite new interpretation of the Gospels is also becoming possible. One can begin to find things in the text that were always there, but never previously recognized; for Christ came so that all the conditions necessary to the evolution of free human individuality could be perfected.

I would like to refer here only very briefly to one or two texts. In the Parable of the Sower, the message—'Who hath ears to hear, let him hear'!—is that the sower himself does not decide what will become of the seed, but the ground. Divine grace does not have the last word, but human readiness to receive it. The 'prodigal son' is celebrated on his return—not the one who stayed at home—because the former has achieved self-reliance. The heavens are, in other words, happier about the one who has sundered himself and been 'lost' than the 99 who remained within group-consciousness. The parable of the entrusted talents tells us that the Lord looks to have more returned to Him than He first gave: the human being must bring the work of freedom to bear upon the grace he receives, otherwise he cannot gain entry to the realm of the spirit. In the Luke Gospel—the Gospel of love and sacrifice—we are told (14,26) that whoever does not hate his father, mother, and brothers and sisters, cannot become a disciple of the ego-impulse, cannot become a free individual.

One could, in this way, find an emphasis on the free individual in all the Gospels. Taking as one's reference-point the addition to the tenth chapter of *The Philosophy of Freedom*, which I have mentioned, it is possible to understand Christ's conversation with the woman of Samaria (John 4) as leading us into the Mysteries of cognitive intuition: this is a conversation which takes place at mid-day, in the bright fullness of the perceptible world; and which delves down into the inner, inexhaustible source of the living waters of thinking. And Christ's conversation with Nicodemus (John 3)—at midnight, when human beings dwell in a world of pure spirit, gaining access to a 'birth from above'—can be seen to lead us into the Mysteries of moral intuition.

The threefold nature of the social organism, as propounded by Rudolf Steiner, is so Christian and human because its underlying view of humanity is of a whole, single organism.

I was once asked to give a lecture on the subject of the European Union. Among other things I drew attention to the one-sided limitation inherent in the idea of 'Europe'. For Europe is only *one part* of humanity, not the whole. During the lecture I said that we need to think in terms of all humanity. However important one part may be, we can only ever understand it out of the whole context in which it is embedded, and through the function it has for the whole. In the discussion afterwards the following objection was raised: 'Of course it sounds very fine to speak of all humanity; but that is such a broad concept, very hard to encompass! Can't we at least start with Europe!' I replied that this was like a doctor suggesting that it would be best to just heal the rhythmic system, rather than trying to deal with the complexity of the whole bodily organism!

Nationalism as a phenomenon of group-identity

The preceding ideas were variations on the theme of the universal and the individual. A further word must still be said about the nature of the *group,* for it occupies an intermediary position between humanity and the single individual. The group is neither universal nor individual. There are many different kinds of group: nation, company, state, political party, church, club, family, association, and so on. But we must ask what the general purpose of groups is.

Groups provide us with an opportunity to *overcome* their tendency to make us into a means to achieve an end. This tendency is characteristic of groups and institutions as such. It is in the very process of overcoming the group-tendency that we can experience both universality and individuality as the double achievement of freedom. If there was nothing to overcome, we would be stuck in a static immobility: there would be no evolution and consequently no experience of freedom as the pure, rightful condition of humanity. The group—and every institution—has the vital task of exerting an oppositional pull against the individual, for without opposition no force can exert and strengthen itself. I will characterize the basic phenomenon of the group in a little more detail by describing two of its aspects: nationalism; and what I would like to call the 'holy institution'.

Nationalism provides an experience of group and community based on race, territory, climate and geographical conditions, and particularly on a common language and culture corresponding with these. Rudolf Steiner has made clear in his lectures that nationalism is very much an anti-christian phenomenon, for it prevents people from finding access either to individuality or to the universally human. It is a kind of group-egotism based on common needs and mutual help in satisfying them. The need, for instance, of the pleasure of speech, is one of the deepest and most indispensable needs of every person.

Since nationalism is group-egotism, we can only under-stand it by examining the nature of egotism itself. Rudolf Steiner's view of egotism is in full agreement with state-ments we find in the Gospels. The phrase 'Love thy neighbour as thyself' means that self-love is so perfect that it can be a model for neighbourly love.

The basic difference between self-love and neighbourly love is that the first is quite automatically present, whereas the second is a free deed. Both are necessary: self-love, as a natural gift, is a foundation, a condition of the neighbourly love we strive to develop as a task of freedom. This means that the dubious character of so-called 'egotism' never consists in self-love itself, but in a lack of neighbourly love. Egotism, in other words, does not go far enough.

Rudolf Steiner says, even, that neighbourly love arises through an extension or broadening of egotism, which thus becomes a healthy form of self-love. If I love all people as I love myself—when, in other words, I expand self-love so as to encompass all humanity—then love becomes perfect. Is the love of a mother for her small child egotism or love? Is it neighbourly love or self-love? It is both. The mother experiences her child as part of her being, as belonging intimately to her. If this is egotism it is a very good egotism, for it has only a beneficial effect.

The widespread dismissal of egotism is one of the worst moralizing stances of humanity. It is crazy to believe that egotism should be done away with. To get rid of my ego-tism I would have to get rid of myself. And if that happened what good would it do the world, or me? A consequence of

the condemnation of egotism, based upon misunderstanding of its nature, is the guilt people feel for being egotistic.
As a result, alongside the first illusion that egotism should
be rooted out, there arises a second one: that we do all sorts
of things for wholly unegotistic reasons. But the fact that we
need to place such emphasis on this assertion should tell us
that this is not really the case.

I have, in lectures, often summed up the whole matter by
saying that there are only two kinds of people: those who
are completely egotistic, and those who have no idea that
they are ...

We can find the solution to this riddle by using knowledge and thinking to make clear to ourselves that egotism—
self-centredness—is the necessary overall consequence of
our past evolution. How could we become separate and
individual without egotism? In the second half of evolution
there is absolutely no question of reversing the tendency
towards individualization by getting rid of egotism;
instead, individuality must be strengthened and perfected
so that it becomes capable of encompassing all humanity
with love and consciousness.

Against this background we can better understand the
phenomenon of nationalism. As group-egotism it must be
viewed in exactly the same way as egotism itself. The great
problems of humanity arise not because of national feelings—which are as necessary and as one-sided as individual egotism—but because too little internationalism is
added *to them*. The reason this does not happen sufficiently
is, as with single egotism, that nationalism is automatically,
naturally present; cosmopolitanism, on the other hand, has
to be freely striven for.

We see, therefore, that from the individual impulse of
the human soul, from egotism, everything which comes
to expression in nationalism develops. Nationalism is a
shared experience of egotism. Nationalism is egotism

lifted into a spiritual sphere. The life-blood of nationalism is the imaginative life of a whole people, through which it is expressed. But this imaginative life itself is a spiritual sublimation of human needs. We have to trace the phenomenon back to this root in order to really understand it.

Internationalism, on the other hand, develops within human nature in a quite different way. We become conscious of nationality through the fact that it springs up naturally out of our personal constitution. Nationalism is a blossom of the growth of an individual who is bound to his race or people through ties of blood or feelings of belonging. Nationalism grows with the growing human being; is part of him like the physical stature he grows into. But internationalism is not given in this way. It is much more like the feelings we may have towards the beauties of nature: when we receive impressions of its beauty into ourselves, when we give ourselves over to it in freedom, we develop love, respect and wonder for it. As we grow naturally into our own nationality, of which we are an inherent part, we also come to know other nations. But we gain access to them through an effort of understanding and knowing; we gradually come to develop love and understanding for them. And to the extent that we can come to love and understand the different peoples of the globe who compose humanity, we develop an inner internationalism.

Nationalism and internationalism have two quite different sources in human nature. Nationalism is egotism's highest refinement. Internationalism, on the other hand, gradually penetrates us as we open ourselves to conscious understanding of others. This fact can shed light on the way people live together and relate to each other all over the civilized world; in particular it can help us understand what factors are at work in the conflict between nationalism and internationalism. (Rudolf Steiner, lecture of 30 October 1919, GA 332a.)

It should be quite evident that factors of nationality will be experienced in a *wholly different* way, and will have a very different effect in human affairs, when they are broadened and extended through internationalism and cosmopolitanism. In the same way, self-love is completely transformed when it broadens into neighbourly love. It is important to realize, though, that the negative and egotistic aspects of nationalism cannot possibly be 'purified' by trying to *do away with* national consciousness, but only by striving to *add to* it a sense of internationalism. The task is not one of negative suppression but of positive affirmation. It is a task of freedom: to sin against it, therefore, is to leave something *undone*, by *omitting* to develop a sense of internationalism.

In this context, Rudolf Steiner formulates concepts which can be very helpful for our thinking. Within nationalism he sees 'need-interest' at work; what is striven for in internationalism he terms 'knowledge-interest'. This beautifully emphasizes the polarity between natural necessity and freedom.

The 'holy' and the non-holy institution

The other phenomenon of group-working that I would like to look at in more detail is what I call the 'holy' institution. We can best observe this, perhaps, in the history of the Catholic Church. In contrast to nationalism, which creates group cohesion through the powers of body and blood, the 'holy' institution constitutes the group from above, from a spiritual sphere.

Christ, the divine Being, wandered for three years upon the earth. Through Him, the divine, the spirit, descended into immediate earthly reality. All Christ's words and deeds were simultaneously human and *divine*. Everything He did was a direct revelation of the cosmic Father, and in harmony with all the spiritual hierarchies. But then He had to step back from the world's stage. He Himself—as I have already mentioned—says: It is best for you that I go. The reason for His departure was so that divine revelation would no longer be *within physical grasp, directly perceptible in the sense-world*. It was no longer to be outwardly identifiable. The task which He left for the further evolution of each individual was, in the fullness of time, *and no less than He had done*, to make the divine spirit human—and thus make the human being divine.

Christ is the Being of the ego. 'I AM' (ego eimi) is His name in the Gospel of St. John. God can only become man, and man God—*in the sense He intended*—in an individual, ego-centred way; in freedom, in other words.

When Christ entrusted to Peter the task of building His Church ('And I also say unto thee, That thou art Peter, and upon this rock I will build my church', Matthew 16,18), He also made it clear that this task was a transitional one, limited in time. For He replied to Peter, when the latter asked Him about the *other* disciple—'the one whom the Lord loved'—that this disciple would take up his task on His return (John 21, 20–23).

The period of Petrine-Christianity was therefore seen by Christ Himself as a time during which the church would adopt a mother-role, would guide its members from without. As such, the church received the task given to every good mother and teacher: to work in such a way that they eventually become superfluous. A good teacher has completed his task at the moment he is no longer needed. But the Catholic Church increasingly saw her mother-role in opposite terms: as indispensable for the guidance of human beings for all times to come. Instead of doing everything in its power to make herself superfluous, the Catholic Church constantly tries to make herself eternal, and to prove her fundamental necessity. This is tantamount to stating that human beings will remain 'children' for all eternity, and ought to do so.

Very influential in this view was the idea of 'apostolic succession'. It was assumed that Christ entrusted only *certain* people with the task of advancing His mission, not *every* person. So there came about an outwardly identifiable representation of Christ on earth. In order to know how Christ works, what He has to say and what He wills, every person must turn to His physical, human representative. Exactly what He warned of has in fact occurred. In Luke 17, 20, for example, we read (in a free but faithful translation): 'The spirit must not be identified with what can be perceived. One must not say: "Here it is, or there". The spirit can be found only through the inwardness of thinking, it dwells within you.'

Since the church made divine guidance so identifiably sense-perceptible, it became—as is everything of a sense-perceptible nature—automatic, natural necessity. So people came on the scene who, ex officio or ex cathedra, mediated to humanity the messages of God. This gave rise to the Holy See and the Holy Father as Christ's representative or 'vicar' on earth. The ultimate consequence of this is the dogma of the Pope's infallibility. Even Christ Himself did not want to be called 'good' (Mark 10,18). He says also that one should not call any other person 'Father' (Matthew 23,9). The Pope is not only called the 'Holy Father', he is addressed as 'Your Holiness'.

What then is the nature of the 'holy' institution? It exists by asserting that people can only be redeemed *through itself*. Just as we have blood-inheritance, so here is a spiritual inheritance: people can only find access to the divine through the 'holy' institution, not directly through their own capacities.

The Catholic Church therefore sees Christ's working among humanity as inseparable from the activity of the church itself. Without the one the other cannot exist. The affairs of the church and the affairs of Christ are one and the same. *Extra ecclesiam nulla salus*—'outside of the church there is no salvation': this is the motto of the 'holy' institution. Whoever wishes to be with Christ must also be with the church. Whoever does not love the church will be unable to love Christ. And because a person's relationship to Christ is a spiritual one, and therefore unprovable by outer means, our connection to the church—because it can be tested outwardly—is made the test of our relationship to Christ. In practice, therefore, connection to the church is made far more important than relationship with Christ. The way that the Catholic Church dealt with many 'heretics' was decided not so much by their relationship with Christ—for that was seen as a more private matter—but by their connection to *the church.*

Every institution as such has the innate tendency to develop in a way that makes itself into its own aim; and to view and treat the people serving it as a means to this end. This mechanism is characteristic of every institution. Whether we are talking about a political party, firm or state, the institution is formed by the will of the one in the highest position of power, a will that wishes to be regarded as the best for all, as a common task to which each individual should dedicate himself. If this will does not appear in the guise of absolute power, it tries instead to clothe itself in reasonableness, by placing emphasis on the advantages for all who abide by it. As long as some real advantage is to be gained by the individual, and as long as this satisfies him, he will go along with it.

In the case of the 'holy' institution, the *divine* will is also invoked. The person in a position of power identifies his will with the will of the spiritual world: this is a holy will, which disenfranchises the individual from having any say about the reasonableness or benefit of it for himself or others. For of course God thinks and wills in quite different ways from human reason. Human reason or benefit has nothing to do with holy will. The 'holy' institution does not require reason but faith and loyalty.

Inherent in the phenomenon of the 'holy' institution is the conflict between orthodoxy and heterodoxy. The 'holy' institution becomes, through its representatives, a defender of the 'truth' which also supports its own legitimacy—in the case of the Catholic Church, the unbroken line of 'apostolic succession'. Those who think differently are 'heretics' and 'people who lead others astray'. One of the most important 'holy aims' of the 'holy' institution is to isolate and exclude such people, to render them as far as possible harmless; it appears to do this in accordance with the spiritual world, for the salvation of humanity.

It is pure illusion to think that one could reform a 'holy' institution *as such*, or make it see the error of its ways. Only individual people can pass through real change, for the human will is active only within human individuals. Any institution arises only by virtue of the fact that people's individuality is *obliterated* by something opaquely impersonal; that, in other words, people stop being free individuals and identify themselves with the mechanisms of power. The 'holy' institution is diametrically opposed to the ethical individualism of *The Philosophy of Freedom*, which comes about when a person finds and fulfills the individual, unique will of his own true ego. The two directions are *totally* incompatible. The official, *as such*, of an institution, is someone who ceases to be a free individuality by identifying himself with the impersonal group-intention and aims of his office. His reasons and arguments about what is possible or not in a given situation will become increasingly 'objective'—that is, more and more orientated towards the requirements of the matter in hand (the so-called 'force of circumstance', for example) at the cost of its human aspects. It is not he himself who speaks, but the 'holy' circumstances speaking through him.

If it is pointless to try to alter a ('holy') institution, what should a person do who considers its improvement vital? He must learn to change *himself,* for the ('holy') institution only exists by virtue of each person somehow identifying with it or attaching importance to it, or supporting its broadening power-base (for instance by donating money). Such an institution cannot change itself as long as it remains 'holy'. It can only stop being 'holy' when there are no longer any people left who make it into a 'holy' institution by forfeiting their individual will.

Such a task, though, is once more a positive one. The consequence of people developing their free individuality is that 'holy' institutions fade. To sin against this process is once again a sin of omission: a failure to realize ethical individualism within one's own individuality. It is only through this failure that 'holy' institutions exist and thrive at all. To labour at changing or improving *them* perpetuates this failure—which is even more pronounced when someone believes their task is to battle against such an institution.

The aims and objectives of the 'holy' institution are no less 'holy' than itself. The 'good' person is expected to 'sacrifice himself' for the 'holy work', also to serve its cause by drawing as little financial recompense as possible for himself; the leading official or representative of such an institution thus embodies goodness by identifying with its aims and making them his own. The institution provides him with the material support he needs to serve it well. His words and deeds are endowed with the gravity of his office. *What* he says is not important, but the fact that it is *he* who says it.

An individual who has not been granted the stamp of approval of the institution is not important. Whatever such an individual may have to say will necessarily seem of little account to those who adhere to the institution. If one of its leading representatives says the same things, though, it is a different matter. The content itself is far less important than the representative's official role. If important matters are to be discussed, the leading representative should speak, for things become important through the fact of his saying them. It is not his individuality which speaks but the 'holy' institution, behind which stands the spiritual world itself. He does not only speak 'truths', but also gives 'guidelines' that can be adhered to.

We can distinguish two main automatic mechanisms in the way a 'holy' institution functions: one is to do with its 'common task' and the other with the power of its office-holders. These two tendencies have a two-fold soporific effect on individuality; one works from within, the other from without. Individual initiative is lost, or at least hindered, by confining the content of people's will to the content of the 'common task'. This *becomes their own will* as far as possible, rather than providing conditions which would enable an individual, free and truly moral will-content to be *added*. This is still not enough though, for the 'common task' cannot—since it is intended to be common and objective—allow any subjective or arbitrary interpretation. Its orthodoxy and applicability to all must therefore be officially decreed by an overall, binding authority. The need therefore arises for representatives who declare the 'official'—that is, the orthodox—definition of the common aims, particularly in their practical implementation. It is only by these means that unity and strength are really assured.

When the 'holy' institution holds large conferences—especially international ones—it celebrates its finest hour; for then the *institution itself* stands at the forefront of attention. As one conference-day follows another, its members increasingly experience its holiness, strength and international significance. Each single person is sucked into the whirl of enthusiasm for everything which 'binds them all together in a common mission'. The word 'I' sounds terribly arrogant and egotistic amid the great, all-encompassing 'we'; like sacrilege, like an attack upon the very core of holiness. For the institution to be experienced in all its glory, real confrontation is avoided. Contrast and conflict are, as far as possible, neutralized.

It is of course understandable that many people feel the need to be outwardly supported and affirmed by an uplifting atmosphere of harmony, solidarity and group strength. But the true ego of each person really seeks help in finding its own centre and strength *within itself*. To the extent that an institution's power and influence depend upon people experiencing it as more important than themselves, it runs counter to the spiritual autonomy that Christ strives for in every human being. Rudolf Steiner repeatedly drew attention to the fact that the Greek word αὐτῶν in the Beatitudes literally means 'within oneself'. The first Beatitude would therefore read: 'Blessed are the poor in spirit, for they will find within themselves the kingdom of heaven'. In the heavens there is great joy for the one who has 'sundered himself' (cf. Luke 15,7). The great joy of the 'holy' institution, on the other hand, is for the ninety-nine who stick together.

Someone who belongs only outwardly to the 'holy' institution, and has no great enthusiasm for it because his respect for each single individual is greater, will not be considered a good person. In the view of the institution, he fails to see that precisely because its imperfections are due to human inadequacies, he should understand the enormous importance of working positively for its renewal and thriving, instead of always 'criticizing'. The external enemies of the 'holy' institution are actually less upsetting than the disruptive elements within it, who always think they know better, think only of themselves and do not want 'to take responsibility' for it. This makes it clear that the individual is supposed to further the 'holy' mission which the institution apparently represents, by advancing the 'holy' institution *per se*. How can someone who does not put the 'holy' institution first possibly be serving the holy mission? He can only do this, it is believed, by representing the 'holy' institution in an official capacity, wholly abiding by its stated aims.

The institution's printed matter must bear an official stamp or 'imprimatur' of orthodoxy. A 'holy' institution cannot exist without an official journal and censorship. The 'Index' of forbidden works may be abolished, outwardly at least, so as to present a modern, undogmatic face to the world; yet inwardly it still exists, and is all the more pervasive. The 'holy' institution carefully conceals from the world at large to what extent its censorship authorities suppress material or alter it to make it 'printable'. The 'holy' institution has official specialists in every subject. Only these people are 'authorized' and therefore competent to write books about their subject. The institution can rest secure in the knowledge that their books will be written from the required point of view.

When something 'slips throught the net' of the censors, there are severe consequences for the staff involved. Disciplinary procedures are initiated to ensure that such disruption of the status quo will not be repeated. The damage done to the 'holy' institution by such an 'error' is seen as far more grave than the fact that an individual expressed ideas not sanctioned by it.

Such procedures, though, nowadays increasingly provoke public outcry from people who have at least some inkling of freedom of the spirit. This gradually makes the position of 'holy' institutions more difficult. They are compelled to disguise their procedures to an ever greater extent. Increasingly, therefore, they assume a more common institutional form, which does not try to prove the 'holiness' of its aims. It admits instead—either implicitly or explicitly—that it is not primarily concerned with truth or justice so much as with retaining power through diplomacy. In this form, dogmatism can turn into relativism. Now 'tolerance' is the key-word. Anyone can write or say what he wants, everyone is free to hold fast to his own belief and everything is relative. But the concerns and affairs of the institution itself do not become relative. The relativity of truth allows the institution's leading representatives to emphasize what must be *done* to organize and safeguard it in the way that is necessary.

Let me say it again: the forms and structures underlying every institution as such, and the 'holy' institution in particular, have not been described in order to criticize or condemn them, or even to allow the individual an inner sense of satisfaction in asserting himself against all that is of an institutional nature. It is my concern, rather, that each individual should awaken to consciousness of *moral responsibility*, and to the clear twofold task involved in overcoming *oneself*. The first self-mastery is achieved when an individual sees through the illusion that the content of his own will-impulses can be seen and sought in the aims of an institution. The second is achieved when the individual stops identifying another person with his official role. The fact that an official himself identifies with his office, losing his identity in the automatism and security it provides, is a quite different matter from *my* identification of him with this office—when I value his role more than his individuality. This may happen because I am existentially as dependent upon his role or office as he is. Inasfar as the institution has, by its very nature, the tendency to overstep an outer framework's necessary boundaries, and make people's individual will abide by its norms, it provides the individual with a *necessary opposition*, continually trying to subdue his true ego.

The institution is the daily, developmentally necessary *temptation* of the individual. It exercises a form of seduction by comforting him with its common aims, absorbing him with the mechanisms of its orientation towards official roles, and tempting him to relinquish his own free, unique individuality. The will of his true ego works daily to overcome this temptation, and to allow egohood to assert itself by combating any assumptions that it is automatically present and constant, or that it is an abstract task or mission. Freedom can only ever be grasped anew in every new, wakeful moment; the individual, specific ego must wrest itself continually from the inertia of what confronts it. This happens when the cognitive Intuition of an institution's true being and function—as the focal point of an outer framework to facilitate the realization of individual potential—is *complemented* by the moral Intuition of an individual will; in other words, the will which a unique, self-directed ego forms within a particular situation through its 'moral imagination'.

It has been my concern to show how urgent and necessary it is to recognize in Rudolf Steiner's *Philosophy of Freedom* the earnest task of forming and salvaging the *free individuality*, which is both specifically *Christian* and *human*. This moral task is the most urgent of our times: the ego-directed, Christ-imbued individuality is threatened on all sides, particularly in places where one would least expect it—in the 'holy' institutions—because the theory propounded there is so often the very opposite of what is actually going on. The future of both Christianity and humanity depends upon this: will each person learn to form institutions into instruments for the unfolding of human individuality, or will the outer power of institutions be regarded as so impressive—because at least they are seen to 'achieve' something 'real'—that people consider them more important than the human being himself, than his physical, soul *and spiritual* evolution?

The only possible path of human resurrection is through positively developing free, Christ-permeated individuality; this will result in the *death* of what is deathly to the human being as individual ego.

The human destiny of Christ Jesus Himself is central to the core of Christianity. He was killed by the 'holy' institution of those times because he wanted the sabbath to be for the human being, not the human being for the sabbath.

After the death of Rudolf Steiner — new beginning or succession?

I would like to add here some considerations about the history of the Anthroposophical Society. The reader who is not interested in this subject may of course omit these pages and turn to the next section.

In expressing my thoughts on this theme, I would also like to emphasize that I respect the opinions of others *no less than my own*—especially when they are the opposite of mine. I trust, therefore, that my thoughts will also be respected by those who disagree with them.

I have gradually become convinced that the history of the Anthroposophical Society has followed a pattern which intrinsically resembles the Catholic phenomenon; and which is based, no less than the latter, on the idea of 'succession'. At the Christmas Conference of 1923/24, Rudolf Steiner united himself with the Anthroposophical Society in such a way that, after his death, certain people close to him came to think very much in terms of a succession. But in so doing they repeated—whether consciously or not—the phenomenon of the 'holy' institution. The consequences of this idea have deeply determined and influenced this institution, *right up to the present.*

It is appalling that certain people involved in the impulse towards freedom represented by Rudolf Steiner's science of the spirit, were—and still are—to a large extent excluded and ostracized. This very phenomenon shows clearly that we are dealing with a 'holy' institution and with the idea of succession. If it did not wish to be considered holy, it would be perfectly content to accommodate people who wish merely to use it as a means to an end. I have been told by some that such ideas show that I do not understand the significance of the Christmas Conference. I have no quarrel with that, since I have also asserted that *they* do not properly understand it. But the stakes alter radically when people who think differently are actually excluded by those holding office and positions of power.

These thoughts have nothing to do with polemic or criticism. They arose through my interpretation of the facts I observed and experienced. Whoever wishes to brand them 'criticism' should ask himself why he does not regard *his* thoughts about my statements as criticism. This would make him, not me, the 'critic'.

In the lecture of 12 April 1924 (GA 236) Rudolf Steiner says:

> For of course the Anthroposophical Society must be something totally different depending on whether I am its leader, or someone else is.

This makes it quite clear that when Rudolf Steiner stops leading this society, it *must* become something wholly different from what it was before. To speak of an esoteric 'committee of directors'* *after* Rudolf Steiner's death, is to assert that this institution will remain essentially the same as before. But he himself clearly said the opposite. For him there is no question of an automatic spiritual legacy passed down through official roles, of spiritual authorization from the past.

Any statements Rudolf Steiner made about the Society and School of Spiritual Science at the time he was in charge of them, as well as the conditions of membership, have *absolutely no validity* once he is no longer in charge. Rudolf Steiner repeatedly spoke of the kind of frames of reference

---

* *Vorstand* (Transl.)

that would apply to a society not led by him, *before* the Christmas Conference, when he was not even a member of the Anthroposophical Society.

The fact that he viewed everything of an institutional nature as no more than a means to an end can perhaps best be demonstrated by the following passage, in which W. J. Stein relates something that happened in the summer of 1913:

> ... then I wanted to see the Mystery Dramas. 'Only members can see them', I was told. I was not a member, nor did I want to join. I asked Rudolf Steiner about it. Yes, that was right, performances of the Mystery Dramas were only for members; but I could become a member for the day of the performance, if I liked, and the next day leave the Society again. So I agreed to that. I attended the performance. Afterwards Dr Steiner came up to me and asked: 'Well, Mr Stein, did you enjoy yourself?' I replied: 'I'm no longer such a fool as I was yesterday—and I'm not leaving the Society either.' That's how I became a member. It is symptomatic. (GA 259)

In 1923 when this was related (in the presence of Rudolf Steiner) at a conference of delegates in Stuttgart, many 'faithful' members—and in particular, officials of the Society—would have considered joining the Society an earnest and holy matter, which should not be trifled with. What must these people have thought when they heard how the 'Herr Doctor' went about it?

If Rudolf Steiner had appointed a successor to lead the School for Spiritual Science, he would have repeated what had happened in the Theosophical Society in 1907, the very thing which he had, *on principal,* so roundly condemned. The fact that he said *he* would nominate a 'possible' successor does not mean that he might possibly have done this, for he could not, for a moment, have considered it; but that no one else—which means *no one at all*—ought to do it. He did not, though, wish to state this too clearly, for then his 'indication' would have infringed on people's freedom to think things through consciously for themselves.

His boundless trust in the people around him led him to hope they would understand: that the world of spirit had— *through him alone*—incarnated something into the physical, which, in prototype form and of initially limited duration, and as an anticipation of future evolutionary stages, had gone so far as to create the outer framework and conditions for an institution whose very purpose and name derived from the spiritual world. He hoped they would understand that it could not continue in the same way *without him*, merely through some earthly mechanism of automatic succession. When it became clear to him that such understanding was not present, he perceived the immeasurable tragedy which would follow his death in the form of objective spiritual usurpation; which, though not subjectively intended, would be brought about by powers of darkness in a still more disastrous way. He could not speak about this, for it would have infringed on people's freedom. An infinite sorrow must therefore have devoured his last remaining strength.

These remarks about the history of the Anthroposophical Society seem necessary to me, because in Rudolf Steiner's science of the spirit I see the future of Christianity, the future of mankind itself; and because, to a large extent, the Anthroposophical Society views itself as the official representative of this spiritual science.

'Christianity is … greater than all religions'

Rudolf Steiner once gave a lecture entitled: 'Christianity began as a religion, but is greater than all religions'. I would like to consider this thought in order to sum up all the ideas

I have discussed so far. First of all, the words of Steiner himself:

> Science as such degenerated, became merely a worshipping of the outer world. Today this has reached its culmination. Christianity provided a powerful counterbalance, a protection against dissolving into the sense-world ... In the Middle Ages there still existed a connection between science and Christianity. Today, though, we need a supersensible deepening of knowledge, of wisdom itself, if we are to understand Christianity's full depth and significance. We look now, therefore, to a spiritual view of Christianity: this is the next stage—theosophical or spiritual-scientific Christianity ...
>
> Outer knowledge and science, in spite of all attempts, will not be susceptible to a spiritual deepening. It will, instead, become more and more a way of handling technology, a means of mastering the outer world. For the Pythagoreans, mathematics was still a way of perceiving the realm of higher worlds, of cosmic harmony. Nowadays it has become an instrument for developing technology and controlling the outer world. Outer knowledge and science will continue to grow more and more mundane and unphilosophical. People will have instead to draw upon spiritual sources. The path of evolution these sources open the way to is one of spiritual Christianity. The science of the spirit will be able to provide the impulses necessary for all mental and spiritual life.
>
> Science will increasingly become technically orientated. And the universities will more and more resemble technical colleges ... The age of rising materialism needed religion. But a time will come when people once more experience for themselves the world of spirit, and no longer need religion. The new faculty of perception cannot develop without spiritual Christianity—it will arise as a consequence of Christianity. It is this which

underpins the phrase which I beg you to take to heart: Christianity began as a religion, but it is greater than all religions.

The gifts of Christianity will be carried forward into all future times; will, once religion no longer exists, give rise to one of the most important impulses of mankind. Even when humanity has overcome the need for a religious life, Christianity will still remain. The fact that it was originally a religion is connected with human evolution; as a comprehensive world-view, though, it is greater than all religions. (Lecture of 13 May, 1908, GA 102.)

In another lecture of the same lecture-cycle, Rudolf Steiner says:

We can ask ourselves the following: when religion is assumed into knowledge, when religion in its old form— in which the wisdom guiding evolution is gained merely through belief—is no longer available to people, will Christianity still exist? No other religion, based solely on belief, will remain; but Christianity will still be there, for although it was originally a religion, it is greater than all religion! This is Rosicrucian wisdom. The original principle of Christianity was more all-encompassing than that of all other religions. But Christianity is also greater than the very idea of religion itself. When the outer husks of belief fall away, its inner core—the very form of wisdom itself—will appear. It has the innate capacity to shed its outer husks of belief and become a religion of wisdom; the science of the spirit will help prepare humanity for this. Humanity will be able to survive without the old forms of religion and belief, but it will not survive without Christianity, for Christianity is greater than all religion. Christianity exists to break through all religious forms; the core of Christianity which fills human souls will still be there after they have outgrown all mere religious life. (Lecture of 24 March, 1908, GA 102.)

These thoughts of Rudolf Steiner about the nature of Christianity make it absolutely clear that true Christianity is quite simply the essence of humanity. The future of Christianity is humanity's future. But why do we need to mention Christianity at all, if it is the human being we are concerned with? This is because the Being called 'Christ' is the spirit Being who, by becoming human, prefigured and embodied in an absolutely real, manifest way, all future stages of human evolution, and thus made them potentially available to every single human being. So we become more and more human by becoming Christ-permeated. There is no other means of attaining full humanity than in the way shown us by the Christ Being. We cannot find our true and perfect humanity by looking for it in ourselves as we presently are; we can only find it in the Being called 'Christ'.

Quite separate from this is the cultural and historical fact that the *words* 'Christ' and 'Christianity' have in the past been identified with human, culturally transient forms of Christianity; and with the limited concept of the Christ Being that was possible given the degree of evolution of our consciousness up to now. This fact has caused many misunderstandings. A reality ought not to be identified with a word; nor a word with a reality. The same things are, after all, expressed in many different ways in different languages. So I imagine that it ought to be possible, in India, Japan, the USA, or anywhere else, to say *everything* about the Mystery of Golgotha and the Being of love without using the *words* 'Christ' and 'Christianity'. In this way one could avoid grave misunderstandings.

Rudolf Steiner himself held a series of lectures in 1922 at the West-East Congress in Vienna, in which it was at least partly his intention to avoid using the words 'anthroposophy' or 'anthroposophical'. He managed this and was proud of the fact (cf. GA 257, the lectures of 28 February and 3 March 1923). The *essence* of what he had to communicate was surely still anthroposophy, even without using the word itself...

The science of the spirit of Rudolf Steiner actually provides us with a wealth of names for the Christ Being, which characterize Him in no less essential a way than the word 'Christ' itself. He can be called 'the Sun Being', 'the Being of love', 'the Representative of Humanity', 'the Son of Man', 'the Lord of karma', 'the Risen One', 'the Returning One', 'the Master of the Bodhisattvas', 'the Bestower of the Holy Spirit', 'the Cosmic Word', 'the Logos', 'the Meaning of the Cosmos', 'the Being of the Ego', 'the I Am', 'the One who Makes Freedom Possible', 'the Perfect, Divine Man', 'the Son of the Cosmic Father', 'the Son God'...

One can also use the names with which the ancient initiates in the Mysteries of pre-Christian times designated the Sun Being who was descending towards earth: 'Vishva Karman' among the Indian peoples, 'Ahura Mazda', among the Persians, 'Osiris' among the Egyptians, 'Yahveh' among the Jews, and so forth. I did not have to think hard or long to compile this list, and I am sure that one could think of many other names for the central, all-encompassing Being of our solar system.

If we extend this exercise of 'freeing' ourselves from particular words, inwardly connecting ourselves in an essential way, beyond words, with the Ideal who embodies all future stages of evolution of every human being, we can all gain access to something quite liberating. Christianity as the essence of humanity itself is not the possession, privilege or monopoly of any one person or group. No one who perceives this 'perfect human being' can be satisfied with what he has so far become. We do not experience our humanity through what we already are, but through what we are striving towards and becoming. Human is not what we are, but what we are *becoming*. We are not Christian, but we are *becoming* Christian. Goethe sums up his *Faust* with the words: 'Engaged in striving's continual endeavour...'

This striving human being is the essential human being, the human being *per se*.

Our past distinguishes us from each other and therefore separates us. The future contains the possibility of uniting all people once more in the communion of an absolute beginning. If what is important is the striving towards something not yet attained, if every person experiences himself as starting from the beginning, then all partake in a universal communion. Becoming human is then the individual, yet common task of every single person. The fact that we may, as a result of our past, call ourselves Hindu, Buddhist, Jew, Muslim, 'Christian' or 'anthroposophist', is absolutely irrelevant in the realizing of our universal humanity. This needs to be especially emphasized, perhaps, in the case of the last two categories, since many people may—either through the name itself, or through the ideas of spiritual science—be tempted to think that Christianity is something they already possess. If they thought this, though, they would only be demonstrating their lack of it.

The perspective of consummation

To give some indication of the future perspective of Christianity's universal aspect, which we can become aware of through Rudolf Steiner's science of the spirit, let us look briefly at the nature and form of perfection which will arise as the culmination of human and earthly evolution.

Rudolf Steiner describes this perfection as consisting of a humanity-ego enfolded in three sheaths. This humanity-ego is the Christ Ego. All human egos will be united, yet at the same time remain fully individual, within the Being of love. In our evolutionary cycle, the Christ Ego is the only possible macrocosmic ego; it is the Ego which encompasses and unifies the whole planet 'earth'. It will be granted to humanity to provide the Christ Ego with an astral, etheric and physical body.

The humanity astral body will consist of all the powers of wonder and awe which human beings will have developed and preserved within themselves; the humanity etheric body, the second sheath of the Christ Ego, will be formed of all human forces of empathy and love; and the physical phantom body which humanity will be able to offer to Christ will be composed of all human powers of conscience and moral responsibility. This threefold embodiment will at the same time be the resurrected embodiment of the animal, plant and mineral realms.

What will remain as the highest substance of the earth when it has reached its ultimate goal? The Christ Impulse was present on the earth, was there as spiritual substantiality. It will remain, and will be incorporated into human beings through the course of earthly evolution. But how does Christ live on? When He dwelt for three years upon earth, He did not have a physical, etheric and astral body of His own; He had assumed the three bodily sheaths of Jesus of Nazareth. But when the earth has attained its ultimate goal, it will be, like the human being, a fully developed being which corresponds wholly with the Christ Impulse. But where does the Christ Impulse draw these three bodily sheaths from? Only from the earth, from what develops upon the earth in the course of the human evolution which began with the Mystery of Golgotha...

Only when we understand this, does the following passage from the Gospels take on its true meaning: 'Inasmuch as ye have done it unto one of the least of these my brethren, ye have done it unto me.' (Mat. 26,40.)

Yes, even the way in which we should outwardly portray and imagine Christ is a question still to be resolved ... An outer representation would have to give expression to the Christ-enfolding impulses of wonder, sympathy and conscience. It would have to portray the countenance of Christ in such a living way that every-thing which makes us human beings earthly, everything of a desiring, sense-bound nature, appears in His face in a mastered, spiritualized form. The chin and mouth of His countenance must reveal the greatest strength, as an expression of the most concentrated unfolding of the power of conscience ... a mouth which gives one the clear sense that it is not there for eating, but to express all the morality and conscience that has ever been exercised by human beings; added to which his very bone-structure, teeth and lower jaw are imbued and formed by these mouth-forces ... From His eyes, on the other hand, should speak the mightiest power of sympathy that eyes can possibly gaze upon other beings with—not to receive impressions, but to pour out the whole soul into the joys and sufferings of others. And His forehead ... would not be that of a 'thinker', who assimilates and processes what is before him; it would, in contrast, be a forehead speaking of wonder, a forehead that protrudes above the eyes and forms a gentle backward dome over the head, thus expressing what one could call awe before the mysteries of the world. The head of Christ would have to be one such as cannot be encountered among physically embodied humanity. (Lecture of 14 May 1912, GA 133.)

In conclusion I would like to mention the legend of Ahas-verus, as Goethe tells it in his *Poetry and Truth** (Part 3, book 15).

Goethe describes how this medieval tale so fascinated him in his youth that he intended to write a drama based on it that should be no less significant than *Faust*. Goethe saw the 'Wandering Jew'—Ahasverus—not simply as a 'Jew', but as a figure who represented humanity itself.

Ahasverus is *everyone* who struggles to overcome self-identification with the specific character of a particular

---

* *Dichtung und Wahrheit.*

The transfigured countenance of 'the Son of Man'
Rudolf Steiner's second study for the wooden sculpture of the
head of Christ (Easter 1915, Plasticine. Photo: John Wilkes)

people, in order to open up to the universal aspect of humanity—which alone provides an experience of true individuality. He is everyone who lives before Christ, to whom Christ reaches out his hand so that he may begin to live *after Christ*. He is someone who feels (in his higher ego) irrepressibly drawn towards the Representative of Humanity; yet also (in his lower ego), the deepest antipathy and repudiation.

In the Middle Ages it was quite natural to place a Jew in this role. This shows that Christianity was simply not yet Christian enough—people thought that they were already Christian, while the Jew was not.

Goethe took up this legend, but certainly not in such a narrow, traditionally Christian sense. For him, Ahasverus was every human being; the human being *per se*. Goethe's Ahasverus spent three years doing everything in his power to persuade Jesus of Nazareth to see reason: to start a family, take up a proper profession, make something of himself; and stop confusing and stirring up the people with his muddled theories. All in vain. So he is all the more furious when Judas comes past his door and tells him Jesus has just been condemned to death. A little while after this, Christ collapses under the cross before his door, and Simon the Cyrenian is forced to carry it for him.

Veronica—an image of the human soul—dries the sweat from His suffering face with a cloth. But as she lifts the cloth above her head, a transfigured countenance appears upon it. As it evolves, the human soul receives from below a distorted impression of the face of the Logos, through sensory perception. When we experience only the material aspect of the world, the various elements of its physical nature, the isolating effect of human egotism, then we see only discord and fragmentation.

But when the human soul can, through inner purification and intuitive thinking, perceive the countenance of the Logos in the heights of spirit, it can experience what Rudolf

Steiner calls the appearance of the etheric Christ. Through the soul-forces of reverence, sympathy and conscience, a *transformed* countenance of the Logos can be perceived in intuitive thinking. From the lowly spheres of existence, the *human being* is resurrected in pure universality and unique individuality.

Goethe concludes with these words:

> ... In one moment the loving Veronica covers our Saviour's face with the cloth; in the next she takes it away and holds it high: and Ahasverus sees upon it the countenance of the Lord. But not the present, suffering one; it is a countenance which is gloriously transfigured, which shines with heavenly life. Blinded by this, he turns away his eyes and hears the words: 'You shall wander upon the earth until you once more see me in this form.' Only after some while does this mighty vision pass, does Ahasverus come back to himself. Then he finds that everyone has crowded to the place of judgement, leaving the streets of Jerusalem deserted. Restlessness and longing drive him forth; and he begins his wanderings. (*Poetry and Truth*, Part 3, Book 15.)

These words give beautiful expression to the experience of Christ's return. It is Veronica—the human soul—who lifts up the suffering, distorted face of the Son of Man, and transforms it into the transfigured countenance of the 'Returning One', of the 'Son of Man' permeated with shining love. This infinite transformation is the eternal work of freedom and of love.

English Translations of Works by Rudolf Steiner (referred to in this book)

GA = *Gesamtausgabe*, the collected works of Rudolf Steiner in the original German (published by Rudolf Steiner Verlag, Dornach, Switzerland)

GA 4   *The Philosophy of Spiritual Activity, A Philosophy of Freedom* (London: Rudolf Steiner Press 1992). Also published as *Intuitive Thinking as a Spiritual Path* (New York: Anthroposophic Press 1995)

58   *Metamorphosis of the Soul, Vol. 1* (London: Rudolf Steiner Press 1983)

74   *The Redemption of Thinking* (New York: Anthroposophic Press 1983)

102   Lecture of 13 May 1908 published in *Christianity Began as a Religion but is Greater than all Religions* (London: Anthroposophical Publishing Co. 1959), and lecture of 24 March 1908 published in *The Influence of Spiritual Beings Upon Man* (New York: Anthroposophic Press 1982)

103   *The Gospel of St. John* (New York: Anthroposophic Press 1984)

109/11 *The Principle of Spiritual Economy* (New York: Anthroposophic Press 1986)

110   *The Spiritual Hierarchies and their Reflection in the Physical World* (New York: Anthroposophic Press 1983)

112   *The Gospel of St. John in Relation to the Other Three Gospels* (New York: Anthroposophic Press 1982)

114   *The Gospel of St. Luke* (London: Rudolf Steiner Press 1988)

123   *The Gospel of St. Matthew* (London: Rudolf Steiner Press 1985)

130   *Faith, Hope and Love* (North Vancouver: Steiner Book Centre, no date)

131   *From Jesus to Christ* (London: Rudolf Steiner Press 1991)

133   *Earthly and Cosmic Man* (New York: Garber Communications 1986)